Beneath the
Wings
of Love

by Roberta Kim

Beneath the Wings of Love

ISBN: 9798390367568

Roberta Kim

Dedication

To the future: Emma, Carter, Charlotte, Willow, and Hudson. With love forever.

Table of Contents

Foreword

When I was a young journalist, I believed in the concept of truth. That a single truth existed to be reported. I've learned since that while some facts *might* be indisputable, we each carry a truth that is shaped by our personal lens. Our innate view of life that we are born with, the people we meet along the path, and our journey's experiences impact that lens. A mix of nature and nurture.

A memoir or a biography about real people who lived real lives is impacted by our lens.

We view what we have been told, or what we learn through research about ancestors we didn't know, through our lens. I have used mine to create snapshots of the lives of Dadson and Ruthven ancestors. I hope the result is a faithful representation of the lives lived and that the telling or reflections contain more than a shred of truth.

Our own memories are likewise subject to our personal lens and also impacted by the passage of time. British author Ian McEwan in a CBC Radio interview (1) discussed this "backward glance" that many took during COVID's lock down. There are dark and light moments in our lives that haunt or stay with us, he said, but none of these look the same at age 30 as they do at age 60. Just as the socks in our drawer will still be unmatched when we die, he added with humour, neither will we have sorted out our life as it will still be a work in progress.

This book would be different had I completed it at the turn of the century when I wrote the first chapter, rather than 25 years later while on the slide toward 70 years of life. McEwan articulated so well why I found myself procrastinating at hitting the print button: it was the knowledge that how I view and understand the stories between these pages will continue to change, right up to my own death.

Can't be helped. Best get on with it. Accept it is a snapshot in time at this point in my life.

When I started out to write this memoir of my parents, I wanted to include the perspectives or memories of others, particularly my brothers. I wanted to avoid a narrow, single-angle point of view. To some extent, I have included different perspectives. But I came to understand, and to accept, that this is my memoir of our parents through my lens. The characters on the stage of my memories may have a different perspective on what or when or how or even why something happened. We'll have to live with that dichotomy.

While my goal with this project was to pay homage to my parents, I was conscious of wanting to show them as a real couple with the imperfections of being human. I have tried to convey the real people behind the labels of Mom and Dad.

I wanted to record my father's childhood memories for future generations. I wish we had a video of his storytelling at the dining room table, but readers will have to use their imagination to capture the laughter-induced tears that accompanied the telling.

I also wanted to give my mother a voice, and as you will read, a stronger sense of her own identity.

Thus, you will read an exploration of the generational influences, family dynamics, and life experiences that shaped the two people who were our loving parents.

As I wrote, researched, and reflected, I discovered the currents that provided the lift beneath their wings of love. While Dad's life seemed like an open book, I had much to think about when it came to Mom's past.

Dad said once that his memories were insignificant. I disagree. I think they were significant because they told a story about the kind of home in which he had been raised. Mom's lack of memories told a different story. I hope the family memories I have selected to share, even the seemingly insignificant ones, will paint a picture of the real Ginger and Murray, a genuine couple who lived an ordinary life but who left an indelible impression on the lives of their family. It was a life of dreams realized, disappointments overcome, and enduring love.

(1) Writers and Company, Eleanor Wachtel, Interview with Ian McEwan. October 20, 2022.

Chapter 1

Letters from the Past

Kim

Listowel, November 22, 1998

My heart caught in my throat when I saw the small, clear plastic case, now yellowed with age and second-hand smoke. I picked it up reverently and sighed in relief; fear my pragmatic mother may have decided the letters were too personal to leave behind allayed. As I turned the case over, I saw the familiar flowing script on one of the blue envelopes stored inside.

Outside, the late autumn air was cool. The apartment had been vacant for over a week now, ever since a fall in the middle of the night ended Mom's brave independence. She entered the hospital on the same day one of the newly reupholstered chairs was delivered. Decorating, always a favourite activity, continued until the end.

November is one of the darkest months of the year, falling between the glory of October and the Christmas lights of December. Now it is also the month that Mom died.

As I entered her apartment, I braced myself to see her wing-back chair without its regular occupant, expectant, waiting for someone to visit. *Did I visit enough?* I thought mournfully.

As I walked through the galley kitchen, my eyes ran along the gleaming, uncluttered counter and white stove top, both unused for the last six months; instead, a tube leading from a bag on a pole into a port in her stomach provided the nourishment her body needed. The feeding tube did its job, and her skin regained a healthier sheen. It was an improvement in her diet, but tears threatened again as I thought about how she had to give up the remaining pleasures in her life, small as they were: a cinnamon roll, a strongly sugared and creamed coffee, and a cigarette. Food became out-of-bounds, but she held onto the smoking, I thought wryly, although her ability to draw on a cigarette was seriously hampered. Bev and I had both lit cigarettes for her during this time. Signs of normalcy are important when one's life is ebbing. Continuing to smoke, refusing to give up her car keys (although she stopped driving), and having two chairs reupholstered were among the decisive actions she took to maintain some sense of control in the last few months of her life.

Next, I opened the refrigerator where a package of pea meal bacon remained in the freezer compartment. She purchased it the previous month for Thanksgiving in anticipation my brother Rick and his wife Linda would stay with her. We all gathered for what would be her final Thanksgiving at my brother Miles' home. It was a challenge for Mom as the aromas of the traditional dinner assailed her senses, and she went home early.

I approached her kitchen table, which held the fax machine that served as her voice when she needed to contact family. She wanted nothing to do with "puters," as she called them. Mobile phones were not ubiquitous yet. Text, yet to be invented.

As I crossed the living room, I looked at the framed

photograph on the wall of my four brothers and me on my
wedding day 20 years earlier. Happier days. It hung above her
chair where the constant cigarette smoke had yellowed my
dress.

I passed the first bedroom where a double bed waited for
guests; her original plan was to use this space as a dining room,
but Mom had not hosted a family meal in four years, just one of
the many things that changed after Dad's death.

Her bedroom was next, the single bed lonely without its twin
companion. I smiled in memory of the family joke that my
parents got twin beds after I, their fifth child, was born.
Dominating the room at the end of the bed was the two by
three-foot framed portrait of my parents, the last thing she
gazed on as she closed her eyes at night, and the first thing she

saw when she opened them in
the morning.

The portrait had been a
Christmas surprise.

My brother Bill had
photographed them and then
secretly had it printed in the
large format and framed. Dad
looks dapper in a gray suit
matching his twinkling gray eyes.
He stands proudly behind Mom,
who is seated and wearing a
black velvet evening gown with
zirconia studded straps and neckline. She wears a necklace of
ruby-coloured stones. She had brushed her brunette hair off her
face, in a style reminiscent of Queen Elizabeth, and her smooth
complexion defies her age. A smile and confident lift to her chin,

a woman loved.

Bill hung the portrait on the dining room wall after Mom and Dad retired to bed that Christmas Eve. The dining room, more than 20 feet from end to end with 10-foot ceilings, comfortably accommodated the portrait's size, but it had the desired impact in the morning. The sheer size of the portrait embarrassed Mom. Dad just grinned: "There's my last duchess, 'a hanging on the wall. (1)

"Kim, look at your mother. Isn't she beautiful." A statement, rather than a question, he repeated over the years when he passed in front of the portrait.

Yes, she was, and Dad never stopped telling her so, although he also occasionally added how he had her teeth fixed as soon as they could afford it. "I got her teeth fixed and bought her a fur coat," he teased. A symbol of success for Murray was affording the things that made Ginger happy.

Ginger exuded a timeless class. When she found a style that suited her, she kept it. She only gave up seamed stockings when she could no longer find them in the stores. When I was a child, her daily attire was the classic 1950s housedress-a buttoned bodice with collar and short sleeves, a belt at the waist from which a full skirt fell to just below her knees. She was selective about her clothing-often getting a local seamstress to make her evening gowns.

A niece described her Uncle Murray and Aunt Ginger as glamorous; in her child's mind, they portrayed a Hollywood-like mystique. An old, black-and-white photograph of my parents visiting Niagara Falls reinforces her memory. At the open collar of his raincoat, Dad's white shirt and tie are visible; on his head, a fedora sits rakishly to one side. Mom wears a fur-trimmed jacket with a wide collar and peplum over a midi-length skirt. On her feet are fur-trimmed boots. They are young, classy, and ready for the future.

Leaving her bedroom, I walked by the bathroom at the end of the hall, remembering the Friday evenings when I assisted Mom in the tub. Something a daughter could do, and she relished the warm bath water. I could see how thin she was, and as I squeezed the warm water over her back and shoulders, listening to her sighs of pleasure, I watched with horror as the water pooled in her clavicles.

Now, I stood in the apartment's third bedroom at her desk. An organizer with small cubby holes and drawers sorted papers, bills, and notes into proper order. I had opened desk drawers, seeking what I now held in my hand. I wanted to close my eyes to think and remember, but family who followed me into the apartment disrupted my thoughts.

"Should we keep these?" I heard Laura, my niece, call out to her mom.

"Let's make a box for every grandchild, then everyone can have something," my sister-in-law Bev directed.

"Does this get donated?" Another call.

I could hear them sorting what remained of Mom's life into boxes, making split-second decisions on what to keep and what to give away.

Stop! Go away!

Slow down!

I wanted to scream.

Although I knew this day was coming, even prayed for it, things were moving too fast. My mind needed time to understand what my heart already knew.

The pieces that remained of my childhood home were slipping away, tossed into boxes for the second-hand store.

What to hold on to now? I looked at the plastic case gripped in my hand, and I gazed out the window at the grey sky, seeing another picture in my mind's eye.

Family is seated at the dining room table in my childhood home.

"May the wings of love never lose a feather, 'til my big boots and your little shoes go under the bed together." (2)

Dad toasts Mom.

From the opposite end of the table, my mother smiles and raises her own glass toward my father. Candlelight casts their faces in a soft glow, and the fruit of their union fill the chairs between the table ends, watching the love.

I looked again at the plastic case in my hand, carefully opened it, and pulled out the first saved letter. I recognized Dad's familiar large and flowing script and can see his hand penning the correspondence from the side of his air force bunk.

"Later on, I'm going to polish my brass and have a shower, then lay on my bunk and think of you. I don't know a better way of spending an evening, since I can't come home to you."

My face felt warm as I thought about the time that I read these same words so many years ago. It had been my childish habit to look through Mom's things as she prepared for a night out with Dad. I had asked her what was in the case after discovering it buried in one of her drawers.

"Those are letters that dad wrote to me during the war. You are not to read them. They're personal," she explained.

"Some day when you are older, or when I die, you'll read them."

I could not resist the romantic mystery, and I see my younger self secretly opening the case and reading, astonished at the degree of emotion revealed between two lovers who were my parents. I could not finish much more than that one paragraph because tears got in the way. I quickly folded up the letter and returned it to the case, vowing never to break my mother's request for privacy again.

Now I had her permission.

She left the letters for me to find.

---

(1) Robert Browning's *My Last Duchess* That's my last Duchess painted on the wall, looking as if she were alive.
(2) The Wings toast may date back to Dad's childhood. According to Confederation Voices: Seven Canadian Poets by John Coldwell Adams, Canadian youngsters who were in grade seven anytime between the mid-1930s and the 1950s have studied Bliss Carman, a much-celebrated Canadian poet who spent many years of his life in the U.S. Bliss Carman (1861-1929) wrote:

> And here's to the night
> Of our delight
> That held the stars in tether,
> When her little shoes
> And my big boots
> Were under the bed together.

I also sourced *"May the wings of love never lose a feather,"* to author Edward Ramsay, who wrote *"May the hinges of friendship never rust, nor the wings of love lose a feather."* On a page of Irish toasts and blessings, I found: *Here's to the wings of love, May they never molt a feather, Till your little shoes and my big boots are under the bed together.*

Chapter 2

Love at First Sight

March 14, 1944
My dear Ginger… Remember our wedding day and the following two
weeks? I think of these often. I think of when Rickey was born, and you
came home from the hospital. I think of how you and Rickey sing songs
together. I think of how beautiful you looked to me when I kissed you
goodbye the last time…Goodnight and kisses to you both. Murray.

Ginger and Kim

Listowel, circa 1966

"How old were you when you met Dad?"

With much curiosity, I pried for details about my mother's life.
Perched on the side of the bathtub, I watched her apply make-
up. She gently patted her cheeks and under her eyes with a
small pad, pausing and turning her face to examine the results,
grinning when she caught my eyes in the mirror. I knew she was
happy to go out for the evening.

Community dances provided a popular opportunity for
couples to get dressed up, the women in long dresses and the
men in suits and ties: the Fireman's Ball, Kinsmen Dances and,
of course, New Year's Eve.

< One memorable New Year's Eve in Mom's velvet gown ready for a Listowel dance. Mom didn't wear a lot of jewellery, but she never removed her wedding rings. She didn't outgrow this gown for the portrait Bill took some 20 years later. She always kept a trim figure.

"See you next year!" I called to them on one Dec. 31 as I skated on a bumpy homemade rink in our backyard.

Up in the bathroom at the make-up table, my mother told me about the time she met Dad: "I was young." Then she rushed to point out her maturity.

"I was working to support my family. I gave my paycheque to my mother."

Children supporting their parents was a foreign concept to me. Parents supported the children in my experience. I gleaned from this exchange that earning an income was a sign of adulthood. That message would become important later in my life.

While she reminisced about this time, I learned Dad started working at Campbell Soup at age 20; my mother was four years younger when they met at the Toronto plant. They both contributed to their parents' households.

"I saw your father at Campbell's. I didn't know who he was, but I knew immediately he would be my husband."

"How did you know?"

"I don't know. I just did."

Such a romantic notion had a movie-star quality, which she later tried to dissuade me from.

"Kim, love isn't like in the movies. I'm afraid you'll be disappointed."

She often tried to temper the stars in my eyes with her common-sense approach to life. However, these stories of their dating years fed an idyllic view of marriage and love in me, and Mom's own eyes sparkled as she relived the memories. In a household dominated by men, the bathroom became a bubble of feminine confidences. It wasn't unusual for me to sit on the stool in front of the make-up table and talk to my mother while she bathed.

This second-floor room was the size of a tiny bedroom and was the only bathroom until my parents renovated a kitchen pantry into a powder room. Thus, we had one bathtub for six people, not unusual in those days. There was a shower nozzle in the wall, but Mom refused to hang shower curtains; she forbade showers in our house as they would make too much of a mess.

The bathroom boasted pink fixtures that popped in contrast to glossy black tiles that went from the floor up, covering three-quarters of three walls. The fourth end-wall, on your right when you entered the room, ran floor to ceiling with built-in cupboards, including the tall centre door that sported a full-length mirror. Behind that door were towels, folded with precision and sorted by colour and pattern, all chosen to accent the bathroom palette. The room's only window was high above the narrow make-up table that sat opposite the sink. The sink was formed from one piece of pink porcelain and featured a wide porcelain surface on each side of the centre basin. Large mirrors above the table and the sink allowed the person sitting at the table to see the back of their hair. This luxury might be the envy of many women, but the most spectacular item in the room was the tub. (Even if my mother did correctly point out that the tub was not practical if someone had small children who needed to be bathed!)

Picture modern whirlpool tubs that fit into the corner of a room and you will have an idea of the shape of our bathtub. Recessed seats were on either side of the tub itself, while a ledge and walls were all formed in one piece of pink porcelain. The structure sat in the far corner, its two long sides against the black-tiled walls meeting in the corner. There were three sides or walls on the exposed room-side where you could sit on the recessed seat and dangle your legs outside the tub. That was my perch while I watched Mom "put on her face," as she called it.

This womanly undertaking included face powder, a bit of eyeliner followed by eye shadow, some tweezing of eyebrows, and her signature red lipstick, always followed by kissing a tissue. It was more ritual than requirement, as Mom had a complexion that didn't need make-up.

Her cigarette burned in the ever-present ash tray, and as I watched, I peppered her with questions about her childhood and about her relationship with my father. To say her childhood stories were scarce would be generous; she had none.

"I remember very little from my childhood. In fact, sometimes, I used to think I was adopted."

Wishful thinking, perhaps?

She noted that her maternal grandmother, who lived with them, raised her. Her father was often out of work, and her mother was ill for a long time. There was no warmth in her tone as she spoke of her parents or her younger years. Instead, she came to life when the questions were about Dad. She talked about how they met, the years of dating, and the early years of marriage. It all seemed to have happened in a glorious and romantic past.

"We used to spend a lot of time talking about our future and what that would look like."

As I reflect, I realize much of this reminiscing took place at a time when my parents' life plans had taken an unexpected turn. My innocent probing may have allowed Mom to relive happier times. I was unaware at the time of the distress that preceded our lives in Listowel.

Satisfied with the makeup, Mom would move into the bedroom she shared with Dad. At the top of the stairs, it was a large room at the front of the house with access to a small balcony. The door to the balcony, which they never used, was in an alcove large enough to hold her dresser and included built-in drawers, cupboards, and closet space on the end wall. This is where she stepped into her dress. Chantilly Lace scented the air, and her skirts rustled as she explored her jewellery box for the perfect necklace.

While I continued with questions, I explored her dresser drawers and closet. There was a black silk housecoat that she wore after giving birth to me and my brothers. I modeled it as well as long white gloves and hats that fed my visions of life as an adult. Mom was known for her hats: from turbans to wide-brimmed, they all looked great on her. She even wore a hat on the day she came home from the London hospital where she underwent surgery. Her sage advice: wear a new hat while you do the housework and then you will wear it with confidence in public.

While we chatted, Mom's advice sometimes touched on marriage. "No marriage is perfect," she announced when she heard about couples divorcing.

"Marriage is hard work." And this is likely what she would repeat in response to this memoir of their marriage. It would delight Dad that we remember them in this way. He was the romantic of the two, Mom, perhaps the realist. "It takes two to make a marriage, and it takes two to break it."

These two "made" a marriage of 54 years when Dad died July 1, 1994, of multiple myeloma. Dad left raging, "against the dying of the light," (1) angry it was over, and that he was leaving. When I stopped at the hospital to see him the evening before he died, he flung his arm out as though telling me to go, to leave him alone. I had been drawn to spend the night with Mom not knowing we would wake up in the morning to the news he was gone. I heard the knock on the back door and came downstairs to see Miles and Bev entering the house; mom was still asleep in her bed which she had moved to the dining room. Miles and I stood by her bed, hesitant for a moment to wake her with the news that would change her life.

Dad was the healthy one, the one who walked and golfed, the one who embraced life and lived in a quest for knowledge. He hadn't even reached his 80th birthday, well short of the 94 years his own father had lived. His death was a shock. The world tilted; everything felt askew. Most surprising, it threw our previously capable, common-sense Mom off balance.

Then, four years after Dad's death, Mom became ill with amyotrophic lateral sclerosis (ALS), known as Lou Gehrig's disease. As the disease robbed her of the ability to enjoy eating, to articulate, to write, or to move about, she recovered the sense of humour we all recalled from our youth. It was as if she regained her balance, lost since Dad's death.

Like a lady who faces adversity with strength and calm, she rose to the occasion after receiving her devastating prognosis.

She put everything in order, including the patio stones outside her apartment door and the new shrubs she asked my husband to plant outside her windows. Her curtains were washed, and two chairs were sent out for reupholstering. Her rose "going away dress" was dry cleaned and stored in its plastic covering. Conscious until the end of her favourite hues and the need to co-ordinate, she requested a grey casket. It was a classy colour in her eyes. Then came a tumble through the night and a ride to the hospital. She did not return home.

I spent the night before her passing at her side, compelled by a powerful homing signal, urging me to go to her. I got up from my bed and drove the 30 kms from my home to the hospital in the dark November night. My eldest brother Rick, living in Virginia, felt it too, and he arrived the next night in time to sing some of the old songs for her. Jan and Miles joined him and the three of them told Mom about a prank they had pulled on Miles. The brothers all left, and a short time later, she left us. And curiously, the tilt after Dad's death seemed to disappear.

When we buried Mom, we lowered the box of her ashes into the ground, and we observed the blue ribbon from Dad's box at the bottom of her grave, as if reaching from his side to hers.

"Mom and Dad are back in their twin beds," was how my brother Jan framed it.

They were together. I sensed this so strongly that it was some time before it sunk in that I would not see either of them again. That's when I grieved both deaths.

(1) Dylan Thomas

Chapter 3

The Beginning

March 15, 1944
My darling: ... The boys in our class often talk about their girls and wives. I was telling them to-day that before I was married, I thought I was madly in love with you, but it was nothing compared to the feeling I have now. The other married men agreed with me. (I guess you think I have gone nuts) but don't you feel different now, Hon? The longer I know you, the more I love you. That does not mean I wasn't in love with you before. Christ, I'm getting in too deep here. I'll explain it when I get home; but I do love you Ging ever so much. I love you, I love you, I love you, I love you, I love you, Murray.

Mrs. Murray Dadson

There's a black-and-white photograph of Mom astride a bicycle on the beach in Toronto. Barefoot, she's wearing a bathing suit, oversized pants with wide cuffs at the ankles, and a belt cinching her waist. She's grinning, young, and full of fun. In another beach photo, she holds a Wrigley Gum poster in front of herself, bare shoulders and legs showing at either end. Cheeky. It's not necessarily how I remember my mother, but this was her "BK" times-what I have dubbed in my life the time "before kids."

In another photo, Mom casually leans against a car looking up at Dad, emotions on full display.

There are pictures of her with various friends, including one in a white uniform when she waitressed at Murray's, a local restaurant. Another is of her in wide-leg slacks, an unusual fashion choice, and she explained Dad had bought them for her as a birthday gift.

Black-and-white pictures of them ice-skating in winter, on the beach and in the lake in summer, and with good friends Sam and Marg Maxwell mocking a hitchhiking pose at the side of a road (with the men's pant legs hitched up to their knees), tell a story of a young couple who embraced life. I could well imagine Mom waking up on her wedding day.

June 29, 1940

Ginger opened her eyes as the first ribbons of dawn spread through the still ink-black night sky. She squinted, sure she detected a soft shade of orange in the light, heralding pleasant weather for the day. There was no rain in the forecast, and the cool spring days were warming. Yesterday had been a lovely 66 degrees, perfect because she hated the heat. The house at 19 Thirty-First Street in Long Branch was quiet. A smile spread across her face as she anticipated the day ahead.

"The first day of my life, the day my life truly begins."

As she stretched her arms and legs, she wondered if Murray was awake yet and imagined him getting up at his parents' home. After their honeymoon, she would live there as Murray's wife.

Murray's wife!

Murray's wife!

She almost giggled out loud.

She thought about the honeymoon and going away together,

alone, as a couple. A married couple. And she felt some nervous flutters in her stomach. It will be fine, wonderful, she told herself. Murray will make sure of that.

And then they would purchase their own home. They agreed she would work until they could afford that. She estimated six months should do it.

She imagined waking up with Murray at her side for the rest of her life. No doubts here. This was meant to be.

As daylight continued to lighten the room, she traced the outline of the white, knee-length dress hanging on the hook inside the closet door. A matching white, wide-brimmed hat sat on top of the dresser with a fresh pair of gloves. Virginia Carol Ruthven would soon be no more, and Ginger smiled as she thought about her new name: Mrs. Murray Dadson.

The butterflies were back as she thought about the day ahead. She reminded herself it would be a small wedding, just family. There was no money for a dinner or reception. Surely, she could depend upon everybody to arrive on time and behave themselves. Murray's sister-in-law, Marjorie, his brother Pete's wife, was to play the organ. Her father would walk her down the aisle while her brother Buster agreed to stand as witness for Murray, and her sister Bette was her attendant. Her oldest sister Peggy would be there, as would her younger brother Larry, and Murray's younger brother, Jack.

She was nervous, but she was ready for this; in two months she would be 21. A shadow crossed her face as she thought again about the afternoon that she approached her mother to ask about the intimate details of marriage.

"Mom, I sort of know what to expect when I marry Murray, but can you help me with some more information?"

Her mother brushed her off and even Peggy, who was married

to Frank, refused to talk to her. She knew there was trouble
between Peggy and Frank, and it made her determined to have
something better with Murray.

She wasn't really worried as she loved and trusted Murray. A
photograph of the two of them sat on the table beside her bed.
The growing daylight now made the image visible, and she
remembered the afternoon they had it taken.

"I want a photograph of us together, Ging."

Murray stopped at the booth and pulled her in. They sat close
to each other behind the curtain, his arm around her shoulders
and their heads touching. She had the best one enlarged.
Murray's eyes looked out in confidence, and her heart did a flip-
flop as she gazed at him. In some ways, she hated the image
because the split between her two front teeth was visible. Murray
was so handsome. His eyes! He insisted she was beautiful. She
had never met anyone who was so good with words or could
express themselves the way he did. Murray was so open with
affection. He told her it was the way his father talked to his
mother. She'd never heard her parents talk with any genuine
affection for each other, or to her and her siblings. Except maybe
the times Mom talked about her brother Buster, she thought
derisively.

Her mind travelled back to when she and Murray met. It was
1935, and she was 16, earning a pay cheque for the family at
Campbell Soup. Getting that job was important when
unemployment was still so high. Her parents needed the money
she and her siblings could earn. Then, one day, she saw her
future. She saw it in a pair of iridescent, hazel-grey eyes, framed
with dark, curly lashes; they were dreamy eyes that held more
than a hint of laughter. She remembered the wave of sensations
and overwhelming thought that those eyes were significant to

her future. She laughed gently in memory of announcing her prediction.

"See that man," she said to the co-workers, nodding in his direction. "He is going to be my husband."

The women laughed at her. One said, "Ginger, honey, that's Murray Dadson. Mary has been after him for ages, but he pays her no attention." Embarrassed, but not deterred, Ginger held onto her belief. It was that strong.

She wondered what those women thought now as she gazed at her left hand and marvelled at the three diamonds centered on a gold band anchored on each side by a cluster of three tiny diamonds. She could not believe he had saved up enough money to buy such a beautiful ring. Life with this man would be good, she believed. He gave the ring to her when they were out in Jack's car; it was raining, and they had to put the umbrella up because the roof leaked. They had laughed as they recalled his first words to her. He had walked up behind her trying to think of something witty, blurting instead, "You walk like a duck."

She told him, "You're lucky I gave you another chance."

She thought now of the past five years: walking home from work together, summer walks in Long Branch Park, riding bikes at the beach, swimming, and double dating with their good friends Sam and Marg. She also remembered the quarrels and one birthday when Murray had tossed her gift in through the front door, too angry with her to stay. It was a very smart and trendy pair of black slacks. Of course, they made up. They always did. They spent a lot of time talking about their future, where they would live, how they would raise their children, and their desire to do better by their family. Murray had goals for his future, and they included her!

Ginger rose to start her life.

Despite the talk and fear of war raging in Europe, my parents looked into the future with a sense of optimism. They spent their honeymoon in Quebec where, for part of the time, they stayed in a cottage owned by Dad's older half-brother, Sydney.

To understand the confidence and security that Ginger saw in Murray, you need to turn back the pages to the love story that birthed him and the couple who raised him in love.

My father and his two brothers were the progeny of a late-in-life romance between an English widower, Frederick Dadson, and a Canadian spinster, Lydia (Lily or Liddie) Leamen. She was 34 when she met this recent immigrant who was 12 years her senior. Dad and his brothers were a second family for Fred, who had followed a grown son across the ocean to Canada.

(1) I'd always thought the name "Mary" was fake, but years later, my cousin Joyce shared a communication she received concerning one of her mother's sisters who apparently carried a torch for Dad. We wondered if she was the Mary of Mom's story.

Murray and Ginger in their "BK" days – before kids! 1935-1940. There were lots of photos to choose from that were taken at the beach, either Toronto, or perhaps from the trip they made north with Sam and Marg Maxwell. Amazing as Mom used to scold me for going barefoot!

Murray is walking along a street in Toronto with an unidentified friend; his rolled-up sleeves show the strong arms that got him in the door at Campbell's. Murray and Ginger looking very sharp, top right. Ginger appreciated fashion, in shorts with a front-tied blouse and in the slacks that Murray gave her for her birthday. This shorts photo is noteworthy as I **never** saw my mother wear shorts. Mom with fellow waitresses in uniform ready for work at Murray's Restaurant. This is the time before five children changed their lives.

Murray with Marg and Sam Maxwell, lifelong friends, strike a hitchhiking pose. Sam drove Mom to the hospital when she gave birth to Rick. The Maxwells lived in Portage La Prairie for many years but the four remained close. Ginger gazes at Murray in another photo and in another sits on the bumper of a car with a gang of girls. Her sister Bette is at the top. The straw sombrero hints at a future love of all kinds of hats.

Chapter 4

A Proposal

(undated)

My Dear Lilly - I do not know how to express in writing the love I have for you. Well, dearest, you seem to be constantly in my mind. If I sleep, when I wake, my first thoughts are of Lilly. I only hope that before long I may obtain some good appointment so that I may be able to furnish a home that I think would be befitting you, for I so want you for my own. During the short period I have known you, I have felt quite different. You seem to have sent a ray of sunshine into my body, and I cannot bear to think of you ever being away from me. Before I met you I had given myself up, not caring what became of me for I felt I had nothing to live for, but since our few tête-à-tête's you have made me feel quite different and it is now my great ambition to make you my wife, for I believe that although you do not love me, now, that in a short time you will grow fond of me. And I feel sure I could make you happy. Now dearest I do not want you to laugh at this, but it is exactly what I feel, and I am fully aware that men in love sometimes make themselves look perfect fools, but I will chance all this for the sake of winning you, for I know that with you for my own, life would be perfect bliss and happiness. Trusting you will think over the little talks we have had and try and find a spot in your heart that will display some love for me. I remain in anticipation, Yours very lovingly, Frederick James Dadson (Irish)

Fred Dadson and Lydia Leamen

Before Murray Dadson, it was Fred Dadson who took pen to paper to express his love in this undated marriage proposal. He wrote the romantic entreaty with beautiful penmanship on letterhead from a Parry Sound resort, The Belvidere.

I never knew these grandparents; she died before I was born, and he died two years after my birth, but they were an influential foundation in my father's life.

Chapter 5

Nobody's Boy

March 16, 1944
My darling, ... I want to tell you how much I miss you and how much
I care, but the words just don't seem to come... Have you been up to
see Mom and Pop lately? If you see them, say hello from me. There is
not much I could write them that would be of any interest. I know they
like to see you and Rickey drop in on them... I love you, I miss you.
Murray.

Fred and Lydia Dadson

As promised in his marriage proposal, Fred built and furnished
a home for Lydia on a lot in the expanding Village of New
Toronto. It was July 1919 (1). Fred and Lydia's sons were 8, 4,
and 3; clearly, the family needed room for three growing boys.

Lot 11 on Fifteenth Street was 50 feet wide by 113 feet deep.
It was part of a farm section that was eventually occupied by the
Good Year Tire and Rubber Plant on Lakeshore Road. Little
Murray would stand on a chair and watch out the kitchen
window as horses pulled loads of dirt away-work starting on the
Good Year plant. The plant was an unwitting part of the
childhood adventures he told later in life.

Fred purchased the lot for $900 (approximately $24,000 a hundred years later), not a small sum for an immigrant starting over. The estate of Alfred Jephcott held a mortgage on the property, and Fred was still making interest payments in the late 1940s. An October 1946 receipt notes a money order "... in the amount of $45.00, being one year's interest on mortgage..." The road in this new country was not paved with gold, rather hard work, and sacrifice. Fred dug the basement of the home by hand.

The family had been bordering at 16 Clarence Square, a three-storey, sprawling brick residence close to downtown Toronto. The three boys arrived in quick succession. Clarence Mortimer arrived on December 30, 1911, a little over a year after the wedding. Four years later, Norman Murray (my father) arrived March 7, 1915, while John Clement was born just a year later August 15, 1916. Nicknames seemed to be common; Clarence was our Uncle Pete and John was Uncle Jack or Uncle Nink-I never heard Dad call his brothers by their given names. Nink was short form for Nincompoop! Dad somehow escaped the nicknaming and was called Murray or Mur.

Lydia gave birth at 35, 39 and 40, ages still considered riskier for pregnancy. Her boys idolized her. It must have amazed Fred to have three more sons arrive as he entered his fifth decade. Perhaps he took delight in the promise of further establishing the Dadson name in a new country.

One of Dad's earliest memories was being pulled in a sleigh by his parents. He had called out "Good night and God Bless" getting a chuckle from passing adults.

"That's what they said to us when we went to bed."

While there was no money, Dad recalled there was a lot of love. He and his brothers were "doted upon" by this couple, who found each other, love, and a young family at such a late stage in life.

"We didn't have any money-no one around us did-so we didn't notice. When I think back, the memories I have of my parents are so fond. Everything was hunky dory. It was heaven," he recalled when in his 60s. Perhaps age contributed a rose tint to his recollections, but the legacy Fred and Lydia left was strong in his memories.

Early recollections were fleeting, such as the one of him and Nink standing together on the back porch with their mom; it's winter, and they are wearing new woollen suits. Someone, presumably their mother, took care to ensure their hats and mittens matched. A woman walking past commented on their colourful knitted suits.

"That's all. I can just see us on that porch, feeling proud, in our suits that were of different colours."

They played under the porch where it was cool in hot summers. Here they had highways, railways, and mountains made of dirt, and they used pieces of wood for trains and cars. There were no toys.

Both parents featured in Dad's memories. His father's strong instincts to protect his children were evident in the stories. One was connected to the time Dad was struck by a car while riding his bicycle. The car threw him into the air, and he landed on his back. Likely the root of future back problems. A few days after the accident, a stranger approached him while he was sitting on the porch. The man was telling the young kid that he needed to sign some papers. Fred was out the door at lightning speed, berating the man for talking to a child and chasing him off the property.

Several blocks around their home were still being farmed, and in another recollection, Dad was on a walk in a farm field with his father and brother Nink. The boys heard the angry barks of a dog and saw the grain in the field moving as the dog approached. Their father stood protectively in front of them until the danger went away. On their way home, safe after the fright, they saw a woman in a field milking a cow on the west side of Eighteenth Street.

"She was Ukrainian and could not speak English very well. Dad wanted to buy some milk for us. She went inside, and she brought out some cold milk and Dad paid her. We drank the milk out of cups. Guess we were thirsty after the dog episode. They are insignificant memories, but they are great."

These memories contributed to Murray's growth from a depression-era childhood to manhood, to husband of Ginger, and to father of five. Those earliest years that childhood experts tell us now are so powerful in shaping who we become, made a positive impression on him.

One vivid memory was sitting on his mother's sewing table while she dressed him, and his father entering with a live turkey which was placed beside him. "It was as big as me, maybe bigger, and it terrified me."

As the turkey story illustrated, they were well-fed, and Dad recalled birthday dinners of roast beef when he would receive 10 cents as a gift. He overheard his parents after one such dinner: "Watch, he'll go buy a hot dog with that." Which was exactly what he did. He was a skinny kid, but they couldn't fill him up. Another favourite meal was his father's rabbit stew, a savoury dish with his mother's dumplings. He also recalled hunting with his father for mushrooms to fry with tomatoes and toast.

It's noteworthy that Fred remained employed throughout the

depression, commuting to work at a paper company via trolley. He and Lydia took an active interest in their community, attending taxpayer meetings and Century United Church. They maintained their mutual interest in gardening, perhaps one topic they shared during their brief courtship in Parry Sound. Fred remained a stickler for proper English.

"We'd get heck for saying 'going to go'. There is no going to go. You intend to go. Or you will go. Or you have gone, but there is no going to go," Dad recited from memory, mimicking his father's British accent. But his father had his own slang. "He would hold out his hankie and tell me to blow my nose. He would say 'here, blow your snitch,' the hankie reeking of tobacco from the plug of tobacco in his pocket. I thought it was a neat smell."

There was discipline. A cuff was administered if warranted. His mother chased him once with a broom when she caught him sucking on ice. He recalled holding onto the springs under the bed as his mother moved the bed in a failed attempt to get to him-with him laughing the whole time. He finally relented and came out to take his punishment. Sucking ice was a serious violation, forbidden after a ball struck a young neighbourhood boy who then died choking on the ice in his mouth. Dad remembered Dr. McFarlane arriving in a Model T, but the child died in front of everyone.

There was also the story of the cigarette butts discovered in his pants pocket and Lydia threatened the familiar, "Wait till your father comes home." He could not remember his father ever getting rough with them, and the cigarette incident "called for high diplomacy. He met with me and Nink and asked us to stop."

Dad described how the family gathered around the wood

stove in the kitchen when they were younger to hear their parents read from the Bible and story books. He recalled one story that was his mother's favourite and the amusing interaction between his parents at its reading. His stories allowed me to recreate one of Dad's childhood memories.

November, New Toronto, circa 1924

Lydia checked in on Murray and Jack, the two youngest, while Pete, the eldest, followed their dog Prince to the kitchen. She looked at the tub of water and shook her head.

"How do two little boys get so dirty?" she teased them. At least the boys were back to sleeping inside the house; it was too cold outside for the tent. They loved camping out in the backyard as soon as the weather turned warmer. The boys shivered as she helped them dry off and get into their nightclothes.

"Take a blanket and sit by the stove. You will soon warm up." She watched them scamper into the kitchen for the time of day they all loved. It was her favourite time as well. The family was home, snug by the stove, and she and Fred took turns reading.

Tonight, they were reading "Nobody's Boy," a sad tale about a boy travelling around Europe with a minstrel group. She heard Fred admonishing the boys in his still-thick English accent, "If you can't play amicably, then don't play at all." As she settled in her chair beside Fred, she glanced at the shiny, clean faces, peering out from the blankets, grinning as they wiggled while they waited. They were never still; Murray and Jack even bickered in bed about an imaginary line that ran down the centre of their mattress.

A stern glance from Fred soon quieted them, and she began to read. This story always upset her. She knew she was coming to an especially sad part where the boy had to sleep in a barn and cover himself with manure to keep warm. She sent a silent prayer of thanks to God that her boys had blankets and a stove to keep them warm. Murray and Jack were silent, hanging onto every word, as they also knew what was coming.

Lydia tried, but she couldn't hold back the tears, and her voice got thick with emotion.

"Oh, harrumph." Fred took the pipe out of his mouth. "Here, here, let me read now." He took over, as she knew he would. Lydia dabbed her eyes with her handkerchief, and she smiled at her boys. Could she love them more? She doubted it.

New Toronto, or Mimico, was Dad's childhood playground. He could ride his tricycle all the way to what is now Brown's Line and the QEW. Dad recalled how his mother allowed him and his brothers to roam all over the neighbourhood when they were young, and he asked her once how she did that without worry. She told him if she wondered where her boys were playing, she just had to look for their dog Prince.

She also told him she joined her sons at the creek sometimes, taking her mending with her, so she could watch as they swam. Living close to Lake Ontario meant water fun in the warmer weather. The kids in the neighbourhood took 55-gallon cans from the Good Year dump, laid them on their sides, and cut them to make tin boats. Broomsticks served as oars and they launched these on the lake on calm days, travelling so far out they could see past the Good Year plant.

"It's a good thing they never tipped over as we would have drowned. None of us knew how to swim."

Dad was 16 when the opportunity to learn how to swim came about. A local man, Gus Ryder, struck a deal with the municipality to teach the youth in the area to swim instead of paying his taxes. This was long before he coached 16-year-old Marilyn Bell in her famous swim across Lake Ontario in 1954. In his later years, Gus Ryder helped to establish the Lakeshore Swimming Club, where he taught thousands of handicapped children to swim. Ryder was inducted into Canada's Sports Hall of Fame in 1963.

Some afternoons, the boys attended the theatre in "the village," what they called downtown New Toronto.

"It cost 11 cents to get into the theatre. There were serials and westerns playing. And there was always someone up front playing the piano for sound effect. I can remember having to tell Prince to go home. He would look over his shoulder, his eyes were so sad."

The boys were full of pranks around the house, which Lydia loved. Dad recalled how he and his brothers, when they were older, lifted their mother up onto the fireplace mantle, teasing her when she could not get back down. This story likely led to the pranks my brothers played on my mother. More on these later, but like Lydia, she laughed, relishing the fun and attention.

As he raised this new family, Fred remained in contact with his oldest son, Syd, who was settled in the Ottawa area. Dad recalled Syd drove an elaborate car which had outside shock absorbers on each corner. Syd did very well in the printing business in the Ottawa area. He and his wife Helen had five sons; father and son were raising boys, some of them born in the same years.

Lydia was a staunch Baptist and a woman of strong faith; on her deathbed, she asked my father to read the 23rd Psalm and to sing her favourite hymn, *I Come to the Garden Alone*. She lived a full life, devoted to her family until August 19, 1952, when at 76 she succumbed to cancer. Dad told me about bathing his mother when she was ill. Her breast was hard as rock, he said, filled with a cancer which took her in six months. A news article about Lydia's death proclaimed she was, "A New Toronto pioneer who knew the district before it was a town and was called 'Western Gardens'."

Fred lived another six years until 1958, his 94th year.

Upon Lydia's death, Fred gave his youngest son the house, which was sold, and Jack (Nink) and wife Phyllis (2) moved with their son Jimmy (3) to Alberta. This young cousin suffered from some form of mental illness, possibly schizophrenia, and his parents eventually placed him in a facility in Red Deer. The last time my uncle took Jimmy out for a visit, he had to get the police to help control him and return him to the facility.

Fred went to live with eldest son Pete, and daughter-in-law Marjorie, in Oakville. My cousin Wendy recalled being a bit afraid of this old man, who often sat in darkness, but who had a jar of humbugs he shared. We now understand the darkened room would be easier on someone with cataracts. Fred had cataract surgery around his 90th year in 1954, a time when the surgery was still developing. It was a huge deal when he regained his sight.

Fred was not an easy patient. One night he got up to use the washroom but, in his blindness (or sleep?), opened the hall closet and urinated over all the clean linen. He threw at least one tray of food at my aunt when he was displeased. The word obstreperous comes to mind, a word Dad liked to use when describing himself in later years. (In fact, Dad did upset (not throw) a food tray in the hospital when a nurse woke him in the morning after a rough night.) The bulk of Fred's care clearly fell to Aunt Marjorie. Jack and Phyllis had moved west while Murray and Ginger were living in the U.S. around this time and, upon their return to Toronto, were soon transferred again away from the city.

As well as three sons, Fred and Lydia left 12 grandchildren. Prolific for a couple who married at a later age.

They lived to see their first grandchild, Joyce, on her wedding day in May 1952, and there's a sweet story connected to the occasion. As Lydia was unwell and could not attend the ceremony, Joyce, and her new husband, Jim Beaton, visited the grandparents at home after the ceremony. The grandparents were lying in bed. Ever the romantic, Fred took the bridal bouquet from Joyce and handed it to Lydia, then likewise borrowed her veil and placed it on Lydia's head. He then proceeded to repeat his wedding vows. It was three months before Lydia's death.

This love my father witnessed in his childhood home provided the foundation for the day he would marry my mother.

---

(1) *31st day of July, 1919… that in consideration of the sum of Nine hundred dollars now paid by the said party (Frederick J. Dadson) … doth grant all and singular that certain parcel or tract of land and premises situate, lying and being in the Village of New Toronto, in the Township of Etobicoke, and the County of York, and being composed of the whole of Lot Number Eleven (11)*
(2) *Records indicate that this uncle's war bride came to Canada in 1950 with the couple's three-year-old son. They were married in England in 1944, but she and Jimmy travelled alone on the ship, so for reasons unknown, she followed her husband to Canada rather than coming with him.*
(3) *Jimmy outlived his father, dying in 1996. Jack and Phyllis eventually divorced, and Jack remarried. His second wife, Maryann Ness, predeceased him. She had a son, Darryl, with whom my parents maintained a friendship after Jack's death in 1981 of emphysema.*

Chapter 6

No Wedding Music

March 23,1944
...I guess, when the war is over and I come home again, we will get used to each other again and forget about these lonely nights. Or will we Hon? I love you more now than I ever have. Yours always, Murray

Murray and Virginia (Ruthven) Dadson

We don't have any studio portraits of our parents' wedding day, but we had a super-8 movie! To us, it was a treasure, and the black and white recording became affectionately known as "The Untouchables" to our family. The silent movie began by capturing a young, smiling Ginger as she arrived with her father in a car at the church. She wore a simple, knee-length white dress with long sleeves and a thin belt at her slim waist.

"My father could put his hands around my waist and his fingers would touch," she boasted.

A wide-brimmed hat framed her happy, youthful face. The skirt was full and cascaded down in front of them when Dad picked her up and carried her across a door threshold. It was at this point in the home movie that we stopped the projector and reversed it, adding the sound: "oops, changed our minds" or "boy, that was a mistake" as Dad came back out the house and put Mom down.

The fascinating thing about the movie was that for most of its duration, the camera simply panned the family as they stood outside the church. We were treated to some very clear and slow-moving footage of both sets of grandparents and most of the aunts and uncles. And a cat that wandered through the gathering. At this point, Mom always rolled her eyes and commented on how there was always a cat. Her mother and sisters were ailurophiles, while pets were not allowed in our home. Mom claimed she knew who would be responsible for them, and she wasn't adding pets on top of five children.

One aunt and uncle were absent from the movie, and their absence formed a family story that became vintage with repeated telling. Dad's older brother Pete and his wife Marjorie did not attend the wedding, even though Marj was supposed to play the organ. Joyce shared that her mother claimed she had never received an invitation. No one received invitations-the wedding was that small. The story took on different legs 36 years later when they also missed the wedding and reception when my brother Miles married Bev Denstedt. Turns out Uncle Pete and Aunt Marj were in town and parked their trailer on the

Friday night, incorrectly assuming the wedding was on Saturday night.

< Dad's brother Pete and wife Marjorie before the war with Joyce, Doug, Joanne, and Elaine. Wendy and David arrived later.

In my memory, we rarely got together with Uncle Pete's family. To be fair, busy families can make getting together difficult and there was a difference in ages of cousins.

Pete and Marj were married on June 4, 1932, eight years before my parents. They started on a family of six children right away: Joyce, 1932; Doug, 1935; Joanne, 1937; Elaine, 1939; Wendy, 1944 and David, 1946.

< Uncle Pete with David, Elaine, Wendy, Doug, Joanne, and Joyce.

To put it into perspective, my mother delivered her fourth son in July 1952, and Pete's oldest daughter Joyce gave birth to her first son a year later in August 1953. I arrived in January 1956, not long after Joyce's second child, a girl, Nancy, was born. I have more memories of visiting my cousin Joyce with my parents than I do of Uncle Pete and Aunt Marj. Joyce recalled my parents were good to her in those years, when she lost two babies to Infantile Sandhoff disease, a recessive genetic disorder.

Baby Nancy died in 1956 but none of the medical experts at Sick Kids were able to determine a cause. Joyce gave birth to her third child, another boy, in 1957, and Billy was two when her fourth child, Douglas, arrived in 1959. By the time Joyce was ready to give birth to a fifth child in 1961, Billy was in Sick Kids with the same blindness and seizures that Nancy had suffered. Jamie was born in June and Billy died in August at age 4.

To compound this time of indescribable sorrow, male doctors subjected my cousin to paternalistic thinking when they refused to perform a tubal ligation because she was under 30. She entered her last pregnancy with full knowledge that it was a genetic disorder and that her baby could die like her other two children. Joyce and Jim raised four healthy sons, Peter, Douglas, Jamie, and Lawrence, but the memories of Nancy and Billy remain strong.

While busy family lives and residing in different communities would have limited the times Dad and Uncle Pete visited, Joyce offered the opinion that not only was Marjorie jealous of Ginger, but Pete was jealous of his brother's rise through the management ranks at Campbell's. Possibly some sibling rivalry. Joyce's own writings revealed a troubled marriage for Uncle Pete and Aunt Marj. Family has learned since that Marj may have been bi-polar.

So, Murray and Ginger married (without music) and within a year, May 1941, they were parents. Part of a generation that came of age during The Great Depression, they grew up appreciating the value of a dollar. They grew up to want more for their own lives and the lives of their children.

They eventually achieved more, but the path held surprises they could not have imagined on the day they married. Before moving on with their story, we take another step back in time. A look into Fred Dadson's past revealed possible influences in his life including a large extended family, entrepreneurial success, and community accolades for his father and grandfather in England. It also provided insight into a health issue my father suffered.

Chapter 7

A Prosperous Household

"… (George Dadson was) connected with the public life of Tonbridge for upwards of 30 years, and in his day and generation did much useful work for the town." - From the Kent and Sussex Courier, 1904

Frederick James Dadson

My paternal grandfather Fred Dadson had strong male role models in his life. His grandfather lived until Fred was 16 and his father lived until Fred was 46. Both men were named George and had large families. They were known for the contributions each made to their communities in the Tonbridge and Cranbrook areas of England.

Fred's grandparents, George and Elizabeth (Cradduck) Dadson, had 11 children and lived in Cranbrook. This grandfather set a high bar for work and community involvement. He was still employed as an assistant overseer and collector of poor rates at 85, five years before his death at 90. The poor rates were a tax on households in England and Wales that provided poor relief, and as assistant overseer, he administered this relief including money, food, and clothing. He was an entrepreneur at the renowned Dadson Bakery and long before his grandson Fred was born, he was a high constable. In this role, he led a procession around Cranbrook to proclaim the newly crowned King William IV following the death of King George IV in 1830. (1)

Fred's parents were George and Amelia (Beckley) Dadson. Frederick James was the second youngest of their seven children, born April 12, 1864. Amelia was George's second wife, his first marriage ending after only three years when he was widowed with one child. George and toddler daughter, Fanny Elizabeth, added 27-year-old Amelia to their small family a year later, and prosperity followed. The family lived at 419 High Street, the main road through the community of Tonbridge that had a population of about 7000.

George followed in his father's footsteps as a confectioner at the Dadson Bakery in Cranbrook. The bakery on High Street was well-known. My father told me a story about a gentleman who came in to order a wedding cake for his daughter. When asked about the wedding date, the man explained that his daughter had just been born. It was his intention to have the cake made at the Dadson Bakery because it was the best. (2)

Fred's father served on various boards and committees, including the Tonbridge Water Company, and he chaired the Tonbridge Burial Board.

In addition to community work, George Dadson supported a busy household that included extended family plus hired help. The England census in 1861 records: Amelia's sister, Harriett G. Beckley, 25, and George's nephew, George Samuel Dadson, 17, living in the home. Also listed were a 15-year-old servant, Harriett Langridge, and a 13-year-old errand boy, George Manser, and four children: Fanny, 8; Amelia, 3; Ada, 1; and Alfred G., an infant who died before he reached a year.

Following this loss, the couple added three more children: George, Fred (my grandfather) and Edith.

Just six years after the youngest was born, 19 years into the marriage, 46-year-old Amelia died. Amelia's funeral card, found among Fred's possessions, noted: "She was a good wife, a kind mother, and a true friend." Following the loss of their mother, a special closeness may have developed between 11-year-old Fred and 6-year-old Edith, the two youngest of the family. There are many letters to Fred from Edith after Fred leaves England.

Six years after Amelia's death, the 1881 census lists 16-year-old Fred as a pupil teacher, his father George as a retired confectioner, and Harriet G., 45, as wife. The couple posted their marriage banns in 1875, the same year that Amelia died. Whether it was from a sense of decorum because this sister-in-law lived in the house where the wife was now deceased, or there's an untold love story between the lines of historical facts, we can only surmise. This third wife, Harriet Georgina, survived George when he died 29 years later. There were no more children.

While the circumstances of his death were noteworthy enough for an official inquiry to be reported by local media, so are the health issues that were an indirect cause of his death. My father suffered from the same ailment some 70 years later.

(1) Published by the Cranbrook and District Historical Society: "The death of (King) George IV in 1830 was marked by the tolling of bells, but the proclamation of William IV five days later on July 20 roused great interest, being linked with the local personalities taking part in the proceedings. We read that Sam Dobell read the proclamation. George Dadson, as high constable, led the procession around the town proclaiming the King at five points, and finally that beer was given away; thus did Cranbrook set the seal; of its approbation on the new monarch."
(2) A news article in the Kent & Sussex Courier in 1879 seems to support the reputation. It makes note of Fred's older brother-in-law, Robert Christopher Budd. "Mr. Budd... had a window that was literally crowded with cakes, which were quite triumphs of the confectioner's art, and we were reminded of the admirable displays made in this old established shop by Mr. George Dadson, who some time ago retired from business..." Kent and Sussex Courier, 1904

Chapter 8

A Thousand Wasps

Cheam (a suburb of London)
May 11, 1904
My dear Brother (Fred*):*
...I hope that you are none of you knocking yourselves up through worry etc. I... think that after all the Dear's suffering and what he must have suffered, no one knows but himself. Dear Father must now be at rest and we must feel that it is for the Best... Believe me to be Your Affectionate and Loving Brother, George.

George and Murray

The local news reported the death of Fred's father, George, and covered the inquiry that followed. This news coverage enabled me to piece together the morning of May 10, the day before Fred's older brother George sent the letter noted in this chapter.

May 10, 1904

Harriet awoke with a start, but not because any sudden noise disturbed her slumber. Rather, it was the quiet. The house was strangely quiet, at peace. It was 5 a.m. and the last thing Harriet remembered was George scratching at his arms and legs, yelling out from the discomfort caused by another attack of eczema. She had fallen into a restless sleep herself, unable to relieve his suffering.

This latest illness had been building over the past six weeks, ever since Dr. Cardell ordered him to bed. On that day, George had been out and about, voted in the municipal election, and even got his hair cut. It had been a good day for her 73-year-old husband, but then he caught a chill. Instead of getting better, the confinement seemed to instigate another attack of the skin ailment he suffered. He had not been downstairs in the house since that day, except for two times, and then only because Fred assisted him.

George told the Doctor that the eczema felt like a thousand wasps stinging him, but there didn't seem to be anything the Doctor could do to ease it. The itching drove George out of his mind, and she was at a loss about how to comfort him. The attacks sometimes lasted two or three hours in the night, with him shouting out in pain and frustration.

Now, this morning's quiet didn't seem right to Harriet, and she rose to check on her husband. He was nowhere upstairs, and after a quick check on the lower floor, she knocked on her stepdaughter's room and entered.

"Ada, I can't find your father. He had another terrible night. Can you help me, please?" Ada was a 44-year-old spinster who had lived with her father's condition most of her life; her presence was a comfort to the woman who had been her mother since Ada was 15. Her father's frequent illnesses were a stress in the household. Now, Ada looked at her stepmother's worried face and rose to help her.

The two women wrapped themselves in their housecoats, and

after confirming he was indeed nowhere in the house, they searched outside. Perhaps it was a sixth sense, but something propelled them toward the washhouse at the rear of their property. They entered the small building and noticed water on the floor around the water tank. Holding each other's hands, the women stepped closer to the tank and looked inside. A shriek and a gasp followed as they looked at each other, hands now clasped over their mouths.

"Fred. Go get Fred, please." Harriet managed to say before sitting on a chair. Ada turned, rushing out of the washhouse and down High Street a few doors to where her younger brother lived with his wife Augusta.

"It's father. He's in the water tank," Ada's voice shook after Fred responded to her frantic knocking on their door. Fred's wife, Augusta, put her arms around Ada and did her best to comfort her as Fred ran out the door.

He found Harriet in the washhouse and walked grimly to the tank. After a quick glance, he reached into the water, pulling on his father's jacket to bring him up and out of the water. But Fred knew it was too late.

"I didn't know how to pacify him," he said to Harriet, out of breath and soaked from the effort of lifting his father. "I know he talked about doing something, but I never thought..." He looked with concern at his stepmother.

Harriet nodded, a tear running down her cheek; "He's chosen his way out."

My father was in his 50s when he suffered from his first bout with eczema, the same skin condition that prompted his grandfather's suicide. I had been helping him to insulate the attic and while the insulation may have triggered the eczema, a look at his family history is revealing. Many in the family mention suffering from this ailment and it is impacting the current generation as well. There are some who say it is the family curse.

To those who suffer, it is a curse, like wasp stings, as my great-grandfather described to his doctor. I remember my father being driven to distraction with the itch. He tried towels soaked in hot water on his skin to stop it and, occasionally, took sandpaper to his ankles and legs. He applied cortisone on his skin, which helped, but it caused his skin to become papery thin. At the end of his retirement party, his right hand was covered with black and blue bruises, the result of shaking hands with well-wishers. Hay fever or asthma, which my father also suffered, commonly accompanies eczema. When we lived in Chatham, the months of March through September were the height for high pollen counts (Chatham is in Ontario's banana belt with the highest number of degree growing days in Canada); during this time, he would sleep sitting up in a chair so he could breathe.

I saw firsthand the terrible suffering that eczema can cause, and during especially aggravating flare-ups, Dad confessed he understood why his grandfather chose suicide. Despite the modern medication that his grandfather would not have had access to, Dad suffered terribly. While I grew up knowing the story of this suicide, the coroner's inquest that ruled George's death "suicide during temporary insanity," shed a spotlight on the suffering this illness causes and the impact it can have on family.

Local news reported that the inquest found George suffered "a most aggravating form of eczema, and this, with other affections, temporarily unhinged his mind and caused him to seek refuge in death." After Fred, who also testified at the inquiry, removed him from the tank, the article concluded in a bit of an understatement, "He was quite dead."

But George's legacy is more positive than this sad ending might imply. The Kent & Sussex Courier listed his community contributions, adding: "He was mainly instrumental in obtaining for the public the recreation grounds known as the Botany Bay Fields." The article described him as "a Liberal of the old school and his religious inclinations were toward the Church of England, of which he was a loyal member and supporter."

Community involvement was strong, but while these men may have set the bar for such service, Fred was prone to hijinks and teachable moments. I'm sad I don't have the personal memories enjoyed by my brother Rick or my cousin Joyce.

Chapter 9

Please, Grandpa

Sunday, August 13, 1944
Darling Ginger…How did Rickey behave on the beach? Did he go in
the water?…Give Rickey a big hug and kiss for me. I love you both and
miss you terribly. I'll be home in a month's time. So long for now,
Murray.

Grandpa Fred and Rick

It is a privilege to become a grandparent and despite their
late start in having children, Fred and Lydia achieved the status
of becoming loved grandparents who created memories for the
next generation.

First grandchild Joyce has many recollections of her
grandparents, including Lydia calmly washing dishes at the
kitchen sink while her Uncle Jack worked on a car engine in the
middle of the kitchen floor. Dad credited his mother's wisdom in
buying the car to keep her teen boys occupied at home during
the depression.

Joyce also recalled walking into their home at a very young
age when her grandpa would lift her onto a stool by the stove
and feed her crackling off the roast and black coffee! Her

grandmother sometimes sent her to the Toronto Hotel to bring her grandfather home for dinner. Sunday dinners with the grandparents were a common occurrence.

Another memory is when Grandpa appeared in his pajamas dancing in the snow in front of her family home, although whether this silliness was a drunken caper to entertain the grandchildren or an obstreperous old man trying to annoy his daughter-in-law may be up for debate.

My oldest brother Rick spoke of the candies Grandpa would share with the children and one memory where a lesson was taught.

Toronto circa 1949

"Please, Grandpa." Little Ricky pleaded. His big brown eyes shone in his smooth, innocent face, and although Fred could not see them, this father of four sons knew little boys.

The eight-year-old was once again pestering his grandfather for some chewing tobacco. He was curious and determined. The humbugs he took from Grandpa's pocket carried a hint of tobacco flavour. Now Ricky wanted the real thing. He looked at his grandfather's white beard and into his grey eyes, and although they were now cloudy with cataracts, Fred felt the pressure.

"Alright," he relented gruffly. He directed Rick to put a kitchen chair in front of the sink.

"Get up on the chair and turn on the cold water." Grandpa ran his hand under the water to test it.

Rick wondered briefly what water had to do with chewing tobacco, but as he watched his grandfather pull the tobacco out of his pocket, he stopped wondering. Grandpa used a knife to cut a nice sized plug.

"Are you ready?" Grandpa looked toward him.

"Yes, Grandpa."

Fred rested one hand on Rick's shoulder and with the other brought the plug up to his grandson's mouth. Rick's brown eyes were bright as he watched the tobacco being raised and he opened his mouth in anticipation. He felt Grandpa's fingers on his lips and the weight of the plug on his tongue. He closed his lips and began to chew. In a matter of seconds, it started-he was gagging and spitting it back out and into the sink while his grandfather brought up handfuls of cool tap water to help rinse out his burning mouth.

His eyes were still watering while Fred, holding him by the shoulder, mopped his wet face with a handkerchief pulled from his pocket.

"So, will you try that again?"

"No," came the quick response as tears and tap water mixed, streaming down his face.

Lesson learned.

Fred chewed tobacco, but he discouraged his sons-and grandsons-from the habit, as this story illustrates. The wisdom Fred tried to impart wasn't enough to fight the addiction. My father smoked cigarettes occasionally; his preference was a pipe. He recalled a conversation with his brother Nink about smoking. He had told his brother, "I'm going to he quit because Dad says we shouldn't. But Nink said he liked it and he planned to keep on smoking." A deadly choice, as some 55 years later, emphysema took its toll.

As an adult, Rick smoked a pipe, like our father. But it was our mother who incorporated smoking into a daily habit.

Chapter 10

Smokin' Hot

March 14, 1944
My dear Ginger... They had a pay day here to-day, but we are not
officially on strength here, and so there will be no pay for us until the
end of the month. When I do get payed, it will be a big one, because I
am earning seventy-five cents a day flying pay now... I have been dead
broke, not even any smoking tobacco... Good night and kisses to you
both, Murray.

Ginger

"Don't (gasp) tell (gasp) anyone (gasp) about my lungs (gasp),
they'll (gasp) make me (gasp) quit smoking."

Mom and I had just returned from a doctor's appointment in
London to see the amyotrophic lateral sclerosis (ALS) specialist
when she gasped out this message. We had learned that her
lung capacity was reduced by about 40 percent, a statistic that
put her disease into sharp focus, but never-the-less didn't
impact her one remaining pleasure in life: a cigarette.

I don't know exactly when Mom began to smoke, but it was
likely as soon as she started working and was earning money in

the early 1930s. It would not have been long after Edward Bernays' now infamous public relations tactic at the 1929 Easter Parade in New York City. (1) The smoking models proved the power of persuasion in human behaviour–and the far-reaching effects of carefully calculated campaigns. Despite no television or social media coverage, images of the women appeared in many news publications.

Mom's cigarette of choice was Export–plain. No filter. This changed in later years to a filtered brand. Her parents smoked, as did all her siblings. When my brother Jan brought his then-girlfriend Kathy Lynn to the house to meet our maternal grandmother, Kathy was expecting someone like her own grandmother-demure, tea-drinking. Instead, she met our Nanie, drinking a beer and smoking a cigarette. Kathy married into the family, anyway.

Bernays believed that by appealing to unconscious desires, such as looking glamorous or successful, we could make people want things they don't need. This nephew of Sigmund Freud's had an insight into human behaviour that was newly applied to the marketing field. It worked. About half of all Canadians smoked tobacco in 1964.

Smoking became acceptable, even glamourous. Advertising promoted the idea that women could keep their weight in check by smoking instead of eating sweets. That appealed to Mom.

"Maybe you should start smoking," she said to me when I was pregnant and gaining lots of weight with my first pregnancy. Her suggestion would have horrified my doctor. I recalled Mom laughing about the summer she was pregnant with Jan. "We women used to play cards in the backyard. I smoked, and we drank gin and lemonade. It was so hot."

There was an ashtray in every room in our house–even the

bathrooms and my parents' bedroom. It was not uncommon to see cigarette burns on tabletops. No one was talking about the dangers of second-hand smoke, and if the minority said anything about the smell, it fell on deaf ears. The scent of my father's pipe tobacco was something I enjoyed.

My mother never saw smoking as a problem. I cringe when I recall her saying to my sister-in-law, newly diagnosed with breast cancer in her early 30s, "Smoking doesn't cause cancer."

With such acceptance of smoking in our house, it was easy for us to take up the habit; only one of the five of us never smoked. I can't recall my first cigarette. I have no memory like some do of feeling sick. My system was likely accustomed to the smoke from years of second-hand fumes. But I recall my first cigarette in front of Mom. It felt like I had taken a step toward adulthood; how naïve and stupid we all were.

My community college students were shocked when I told them I smoked in my university classes in the 70s, as did some of my professors while they were teaching. My students would have been further stunned if they could have seen, as I did on a visit to my 80-year-old grandmother's nursing home, my mother and aunt take her out onto the porch to sneak a cigarette. The home had banned smoking because someone had suffered a burn.

Smoking was ubiquitous. In restaurants, bars, hospitals, and workplaces. Mom never quit. The day she begged me to not tell anyone about her lungs, I assured her. "Don't worry, Mom. No one is going to tell you to quit. It isn't the smoking that got you."

In an ironic twist, it was public relations campaigns that turned the tide on society's attitudes about smoking. In the late 70s, pregnant women were targeted and then campaigns grew through the 80s and 90s to include activists and movements to boycott cigarette companies.

I tried quitting, more than once. In 1981, the televised funeral of Terry Fox inspired me. Terry is a Canadian hero who raised money to fight cancer by running across the country after losing one leg to the disease. It took me two years before I had any success, and then it was my pregnancy that motivated me. Quitting became a socially acceptable course of action. "Cigarettes cause cancer" was the new slogan, much to my mother's chagrin.

But smoking was part of the social fabric for my parents, their friends, and society as they began married life in their first home.

(1) *The father of public relations arranged for glamorous women to walk in the parade while they smoked cigarettes, or as he had dubbed them, "Torches of Freedom." His client, the American Tobacco Company, wanted to increase sales, specifically by targeting women.*

Chapter 11

The Fourth Street Knitting Gang

March 16, 1944
… How do you like working at the A&P. Don't do too much lugging around. You mentioned something about lugging things around in your last letter. How do they treat you over there? I guess you will be meeting people you know all day long… P.S. I love you. Murray.

Dadsons, Maxwells & Gimblets

After the wedding, Ginger worked for six months making bullets at a munitions factory on Lakeshore Drive to help earn a down payment on a house. She and Murray could move out of Lydia and Fred's home. A tiny house at 111 Fourth Street

became their home, the first of six, but on the day the furniture arrived at this first home, Ginger sat in the middle of the living room floor and cried because she thought it was too big to fit the small rooms.

< 111 Fourth Street, "a little nest that's nestled where the roses bloom…"

"We spent some of our best years in that little house," Dad reflected years later. Even if for the first few years, it involved some sacrifice on both their parts. During the time Dad spent in RCAF training in New Brunswick and Prince Edward Island, it was this home where Mom and Rick waited. She took on different part-time jobs to help make ends meet.

Today, parents buy homes expecting their two or three children will each have their own bedrooms, but the two-bedroom bungalow on Fourth Street eventually filled with six people-two adults and four boys. Frederick Murray (Rick) arrived on May 3, 1941.

May 2, 1941

"We're going to have a baby," Murray and Bette were singing and dancing while Ginger watched, partly grinning and partly wincing as she felt the contractions. As her husband and sister danced a two-step around the living room, Ginger tried to tap down the fear she was feeling. "I'm the one having the baby," she thought as she watched them dance, fearful at what lay ahead, but happy to be at this point. Her expanded girth dismayed her.

Out loud, she called: "Murray, you have to call Sam."

Pre-arranged, Sam Maxwell had happily agreed to chauffeur her to St. Jo's when the time came. He and Marg already had two boys and they were delighted their friends would join them in parenthood. Murray stopped dancing long enough to make the call and promised Ginger that her chariot was on its way.

As Sam pulled into the driveway, Murray picked up the small suitcase and helped his wife out of the chair. At the door, he wrapped his arms lovingly around her swollen body, whispering in her ear, "God, I love you, Ging."

He got her seated in the passenger seat and placed the

suitcase in the trundle.

"Marg sends her love, Ginger," Sam said as they left.

Ginger was quiet for a few minutes, resting and trying to remain calm. Suddenly, she knew what she needed and knowing the nuns at St. Joseph's Hospital would not allow her to smoke, she asked.

"Sam, can you pull over? My cigarettes are in my bag."

Sam held his pipe between his teeth and pulled the car over.

There was a second pregnancy following Rick's birth that ended in miscarriage and then a war intervened, so it was six years later, April 2, 1947, that William Mark (Bill) was born. Next came Jan Paul on Oct. 3, 1950, and then Miles Peter on July 26, 1952, all born while my parents lived on Fourth Street.

After the war, Ginger took charge of the expanding household and Murray focused on his career at Campbell's. Lifelong friendships formed, most notably with a couple across the street, Ross and Phyllis Gimblet, Uncle Ross and Aunt Phyl to us kids, part of our family. Ross was a renowned lacrosse player in his youth. Aunt Phyl was an Avon Lady and a busy one if the number of orders that covered her dining room table and hutch were an indication.

Very cultured and well-read, they regularly attended theatre including openings at Stratford. Aunt Phyl called me at my university residence one snowy night in 1977. "I have an extra ticket to see a play at the Royal Alexandra. Can you meet me there?" You bet, and I was lucky to be part of an audience to see Yul Brenner in what became a signature role for him in "The King and I." I do recall feeling a bit out of my element standing with Aunt Phyl in the lobby as she enjoyed a drink before the play!

On one occasion they dropped in unexpectedly when we

were living in Listowel; our parents were away. In an act that demonstrated how familiar they were with each other, Phyl wrote a brief message to Mom in the dust on one of the tables! Mom was not impressed.

I visited Aunt Phyl in 2006 in her nursing home.

"Rick is the reason we met," Aunt Phyl told me about her friendship with Mom. "I was sitting in the backyard reading and this little kid comes around the corner. We had a teeter totter there for Barry. The kid comes up and gets on it, so with my one foot, I provided the weight at the other end to raise him up. I was doing this and then something happened, and the teeter totter hit him in the face, and he was crying. This woman came running around the corner of the house, and I thought, 'oh boy, I'm going to get it now' but she was fine with it, and we just struck up a conversation, and we hit it off."

With just one son, Barry, the Gimblet's home was a much quieter household, except on the one occasion that Aunt Phyl laughingly recounted. She was relaxed on the front porch in the early evening and saw a child running up the street with no clothes on. She was feeling smug that she had tucked her son into his bed until the running child came into focus, and she realized he belonged to her!

Uncle Ross enjoyed telling another story about how he sometimes came home to find Murray in his home, resting flat on his back on the living room floor, reading Time magazine.

< Ross and Phyl Gimblet

"And he would be humming. He wouldn't knock at the door or anything. He'd just come in and lay down." Ross would grin at the memory.

"Just to find some peace. You know your parents had a full household with you kids in those days."

The women had their own way of getting out of the house. Mom and Phyl began with three other women, Anne Murdoch, Marj Carr, and Nell (?), what they called the Fourth Street Knitting Gang. They really did knit baby layettes. But Phyl and Mom were not women to be defined entirely by the womanly pursuits of cooking, cleaning, and knitting. The Fourth Street Knitting Gang soon began playing poker and enjoying a gin and lemonade. The host added cheese and crackers and each player threw in $1. Occasionally, they used the pot to treat themselves to dinner. They also attended the horse races at Long Branch Racetrack.

"When we were hard up, we went to the last two races, which were free," Aunt Phyl recalled. "Your father went with us once. You could walk around and see the horses. Your father looked glum. He could not stand the rubbish because attendees covered the ground with their losing tickets."

My parents held parties in this first home where Dad recounted a bit of fun. The wall between the kitchen and the dining room had a small pass-through. It was a big joke to lift my mother up and pull her through the hole in the wall-she was slight enough to fit when she wasn't pregnant! The parties and the poker games included alcohol, but Dad said there was very little drinking. One year there was a beer strike, and friends could not believe it when Dad found a case of beer in the basement that he had put there and forgotten about.

Murray and Ginger were creating lots of memories in their

first home, but a fourth baby was too much for a two-bedroom home. Soon after Miles' birth in 1952, they made a move to a newer home on Courtland Crescent in the new subdivision Applewood Acres. It became the first of many moves the family experienced over the next few years. Courtland was where my cousin Sharon lived with us for a while, but it was years before I learned the secret behind this. The family was only in this new house for a few short months when a promotion and a job transfer to the United States changed lives.

Moving a family of four children from Canada to the U.S. was a momentous adventure for my parents, although it was perhaps minor when set against the courage of ancestors who crossed oceans and changed the course of their lives. Fred's bold decision to cross the Atlantic in his late 40s is intriguing. He left behind what had been a full life, one that included marriage and fatherhood.

Chapter 12

Fred's First Marriage

"26 day of July 1909
"This is to certify that F. Dadson of 3 Yardley Terrace, Tonbridge, was
this day duly elected a member of this our Argyle Lodge and regularly
initiated into the Mysteries of Druidism."

Fred and Augusta (Wise) Dadson

My grandfather's Ancient Order of Druid membership certificate from 1909 was among papers he brought to Canada. Whether membership was a distraction, or if he was seeking solace the month following his first wife's death, remains a mystery. Just as the details around his first marriage created some speculation.

The 1891 England census lists 28-year-old Fred and 6-year-old Sidney (sic) Dadson as borders in a household headed by a widow Augusta Wise, 42. There are four daughters and three sons also listed. The older daughters are dressmakers while the youngest, Adela, is age 11 and a scholar - a term for children still in school. The sons are all clerks. This family resulted from the marriage between Stanley L. Wise and Augusta Tompsett; Augusta was widowed in 1882.

Ten years later, the 1901 census lists Augusta and Fred as husband and wife, with Sidney as their son. No one else is in the household.

It is unclear why Augusta and Fred were not married earlier. Their son was conceived after Augusta was widowed so he was not the product of an illicit affair. There is family speculation that Fred's father did not approve of the union. There is also evidence that Stanley Wise left Augusta in comfortable financial circumstances. Perhaps she did not see a need to hurry into marriage. There was also some family speculation that Sidney was the child of one of Augusta's daughters and not Augusta. However, if that was the case, why wouldn't he marry the daughter? It would not have been the first hastily arranged marriage of the time. The eldest daughter, 17, was of marriageable age. It's also plausible, and I am inclined to believe, that Augusta indeed gave birth to Sydney in her late 30s, the result of a union with Fred, in his early 20s.

Perhaps great-grandfather George didn't approve of his son marrying an older woman. Our society still questions such May-December unions, particularly when it is the man who is younger-why would anyone choose an older woman, seems to be the question. It's entirely conjecture, but Fred was only 11 when he lost his mother; perhaps an older woman provided a sense of security or stability he searched for in his life. His second spouse, my grandmother, was younger than him, but her 35 years would differ greatly from someone in her 20s. I posit it was her maturity that was part of the attraction.

Further research into Augusta's estate dispels another family idea that Fred spent his wife's fortune before coming to Canada. A Probate Calendar shows that on death, Augusta's effects were 575 pounds, eightpence, a sizeable amount of money in 1909.

The sum equaled approximately four years of wages for a skilled labourer. Her will directed 100 pounds to son Sidney (sic) Frederick of Ottawa, Canada; 200 pounds to daughter Adela Wise; and 200 pounds, plus any residue, to son Stanley Herbert Wise of Southampton. Nothing to her husband. Perhaps it was Syd's 100 pounds, equal to about a year's wages, that helped finance Fred's emigration; that sum would have covered Fred's second-class ticket and any living expenses until he settled and secured employment. He would also have his own resources, from his work at a printing company and his own family.

What I can confirm is that Fred's father George died in May 1904, his son Syd left for New York in 1907, and his wife Augusta died in June 1909. No parents, his only child gone, and his wife deceased. It isn't surprising that five months later in November Fred followed Sydney across the ocean. Syd had first landed in New York but soon made his way to Canada, marrying in February 1909 and settling in the Ottawa area working as an accountant.

Fred's future lay living closer to his son, and he joined many of his fellow countrymen, who were setting their sights on a new start in a new country called Canada.

Chapter 13

Immigration in the 1900s

1926, Nottingham, England
"My Dear Brother and Sister (Fred and Lydia)…thank you for your note and photos… you all look a very happy family, yours are all boys, and mine all girls…my youngest will be 19 in May, you remember pushing her in the push chair, that is a long time ago, isn't it, how time flies… by the way I should like your dog, everybody admired him… we often talk about you and wonder how you are doing… I wonder if you will ever come to England again, it is a long journey… Your affectionate sister and brother Edith and Ted."

Fred

Around the turn of the 20th century, when people emigrated from their homeland, most left with the understanding they would never see family again. It was not a simple or easy decision to leave everything familiar behind, and the journey itself involved many days or weeks of travel. Jumping onto a plane to return within hours was not an option. Letters written by Fred's family, as above, reflect how much they missed him. With the help of what I have been told, family letters, records, and websites, I imagine the day he left for Canada.

Nov. 5, 1909

"Hey, mister. Guess what? We're going to go to Canada."

Fred stood at the ship's railing, watching the children play behind him as their parents kept an eye. One of them had stopped to make this exciting proclamation to one of the other passengers. Everyone chuckled at the youthful exuberance while in his mind, Fred corrected the youngster as he would have a pupil in the past. "You are not going to go. You are either going or you are not, but you are not going to go." However, these young parents might not appreciate his insistence on proper use of the English language on this first of many days at sea. He imagined making this voyage with Sydney at the same age and shook his head. He turned instead to look out at the Liverpool port below, bustling with activity.

Taking a deep breath of the cold and salty maritime air, he reflected on the long trip north from Tonbridge and the emotional goodbyes with family. Edith, of course, had tears. Working to keep his own emotions in check as he thought of his sister, he distracted himself by watching the deliveries of food for the voyage and the distribution of passenger trunks, like his own, which kept employees of the Allan Steamship Co. occupied.

A slight man of medium height, Fred dressed formally for this momentous occasion, wearing a black coat and top hat. Aware of the gray that sprinkled his beard, he was conscious of his 45 years. While looking forward to seeing Syd again, he was both anxious and sombre. It made perfect sense for someone at Syd's age to leave England for a better future, but was approaching 50 a little late to start over? He thought back to the past summer, one of the coldest he could remember, beginning with Augusta's death in June. June's lack of sunshine seemed to match the mood of the household. While he mourned her passing, he had not hesitated to begin arrangements to follow Syd to Canada. Augusta's family and his own siblings were busy with their own lives. He believed he would be better off living in the same country as his son, who had encouraged him to follow. Syd wrote of an exciting voyage and the work he readily found in the Ottawa area. His life was unfolding for him-he had married, and Fred was eager to meet his new daughter-in-law. Perhaps there would be grandchildren in his future.

Fred pulled a pamphlet out of his pocket and read again the information printed by the Allan Steamship Co. which was contracted by the new Canadian government to bring immigrants to its shores:

"The climate is particularly healthy, the proportion of deaths to the population, according to a recent return, being only 1 in 98, as compared with 1 in 74 in the United States, 1 in 46 in England, 1 in 42 in France, and 1 in 40 in Germany. Nearly 6,000 miles of Railway are already in operation, and 2,000 miles are in course of construction. Extensive additional Canal Works are (sic) also in course of construction, affording the prospect of large demand for ... Labourers." (1)

The flyer promoted the route the ship traveled, "first through the Gulf, and then through the magnificent River St. Lawrence."

Pocketing the flyer and determined to look forward, not back, Fred squared his shoulders and strode off to find his stateroom and assigned berth. He found a lower bunk with a curtain he could pull across for privacy and to shut out light. A sink in the room permitted simple wash ups. He was a little dismayed his berth was on the upper deck and hoped that would not lead to seasickness. He hoped he would be like Syd and not suffer any of that. At least the room was close to the middle of the ship. Another gentleman entered the room, taking the other assigned *berth on top. Fred greeted him.*

"How do you do, sir. Allow me to introduce myself. Mr. Frederick Dadson of Tonbridge." He offered his hand. "It looks like we will be sea mates for the voyage."

*"Hello Mr. Dadson. A pleasure to meet you, I'm sure. I'm Mr. *Frank Sargeant."*

The gentlemen exchanged further pleasantries and decided to tour the ship to get out of the small cabin. As Second Cabin Passengers, the men could use the music room and the dining salon with its shining teak finish of paneled walls and padded furniture. They stopped in the Smoking Room to enjoy a pipe sitting on the padded booth seats under a skylight. Soon, with a drink in hand, Fred found he was pleasantly anticipating this next adventure in life.

The website 'British Immigrants in Montreal' reports that "in 1902 the greatest influx of immigrants in Canada's history began and continued until the beginning of World War 1 in 1914." With a growing population in England and a decline in opportunities or advancements, Canada looked appealing and people, like Fred, were leaving.

The Corsican that Fred traveled on was one of three steamships built by the Allan Royal Mail Line in 1907 that sailed within six months of each other. (2)

Fred's eight-day second-cabin journey would have cost him in the neighbourhood of $50 or roughly 29 pounds in 1901 for a shared stateroom with two berths. In 2022, a transatlantic trip by ship with meals would be about $1,600.00 at the lower end. Fred shared Room 83 with a Mr. F. Sargeant according to the names of passengers published in a booklet that Fred kept after arriving in Canada.

My grandfather and his fellow 209 Second Cabin Passengers

ate well. (3) They arrived in Montreal on Nov. 13 after a journey that lasted two days longer than the advertised six. These trips were not without some risk. An iceberg damaged the Corsican three years after Fred's voyage, in 1912, the same year the Titanic sank off the shores of eastern Canada. Then, the Corsican was ship-wrecked near Cape Race, Newfoundland, in 1923.

Even for the second-class or second-cabin passenger, the voyage was a rare pleasure. Syd was in his early 20s when he left England, and his letters home likely helped Fred make his own decision. One of Syd's letters, written two years before Fred left, was addressed to an Edie, (perhaps Adela Wise, his half-sister). Syd signed the letter, Your affect. Brother Syd. About his trip to New York, he wrote:

"Just a few lines, as promised. I arrived in New York on the 4th after a most enjoyable voyage, have never had such a good time before, had lots of fun on board. There were only 96 second-class passengers which were all very nice people. We had two dances and a concert every night, all of which were left to me to arrange, so you can guess I was all there. Every night some of us would stop on deck til between 3 and 4 in the morning, smoking and spinning yarns, etc. I was quite sorry when I arrived, because I had not been a bit sick, in fact could have done with another month of it."

Syd did not stay south of the Canadian border. In the same letter, he complains about the work he is doing at a mill which is *"very rough and dirty and does not agree with my asthma, which I have had every day, so (I) shall soon quit."*

Syd moved to Canada, settling in the Ottawa area. He married fellow accountant Florence Elizabeth Barbara, who hailed from Winnipeg, Manitoba, in February 1909. The marriage ended

Roberta Kim

sadly when Florence died in 1911 of pulmonary tuberculosis. The 1911 Canadian census lists Syd as a 26-year-old widower and accountant, lodging at a home on Waverly Street in Ottawa. Syd married again in 1912 to Helen Mary Macdonald.

My parents honeymooned at Syd's cottage in Quebec after their marriage in 1940. We knew about Dad's older half-brother, but never met him. Syd died in 1965 at 80.

Fred maintained correspondence with his English family, and he kept a few of their letters among his papers.

As this chapter's letter to Fred and Lydia from his sister reflects, leaving family behind to begin a new life leaves holes in the lives of those left behind. In the 1900s, the decision to move to another country came without benefit of social media to keep in touch. Letters sent through the mail took many weeks or even months to arrive. Fred's sister Edith appeared to have been a faithful correspondent, subtly chastising Fred for his lack of communication; *"it seems ages since we heard anything of you... we often talk about you and wonder how you are... I have written two letters to you at different times, but think they must have gone to the bottom..."*

It was left to such correspondence to share sad news as well. His sister Minnie (the family's name for the oldest sister Amelia) also wrote to him from her home on the Isle of Wight, *"I must tell you our dear sister Ada passed on..."* Amelia was living with her son Walter Adolph Budd, whom she called by his second name *"... Adolph is keeping very busy it being the season for the Island."*

Ada's widowed husband wrote to Fred in 1939, *"The time we are living in now is not much for anyone. I hope this awful war will come to a speedy finish and Hitler and all his war lords will be absolutely crushed for all time..."*

Before leaving England, Fred secured a reference from his employer, the International Paper Company, 179 Queen Victoria Street, London, England. (4) It would have been a valuable ticket to finding work when he landed in Canada and likely helped him secure employment at the Dominion Paper Box Company in Toronto.

Fred arrived in Quebec in November, and the assumption is he contacted his son, and stayed with Sydney and his wife through Christmas 1909 and the early winter months of 1910. At some point, Fred traveled to a resort in Parry Sound. Perhaps he was seeking a mate, following in the footsteps of his father and grandfather who each quickly remarried after their wives died. If he did indeed have doubts about immigrating to Canada at his age, he was in for a pleasant surprise, as life had much in store for him yet.

While Fred was dealing with the aftermath of many personal losses in England, Lydia Leamen, an independent spinster, part of a family of early settlers in Toronto, was going about her own life in Canada. Light was shed on the path this future mother of Dad's took toward meeting Fred, thanks to another letter.

(1) Norway Heritage Hands Across the Sea: http://www.norwayheritage.com/ p_shiplist.asp?co=allan
* Fred's mate was F. Sargeant. We don't have his actual first name.
(2) This 10,000-ton ship had room for 208 First Class, 298 Second and 1,000 Third Class passengers. They equipped it with electricity, a ventilation system, and a Marconi Radio. Its top speed was 16 knots.
(3) A sample menu included strawberries, porridge, eggs, ham, sausage, potatoes, and baked goods for breakfast; beef steak pie, roast beef, potatoes, rice and pudding or tart for lunch; and for dinner soup, rabbit stew, beef, turkey, potatoes, and cauliflower, followed by plum pudding with brandy, or apple pie and ice cream and cheese.
(4) "He is familiar with the various branches of receiving and delivering and has performed his duties with every satisfaction to us, so we can recommend him to a similar position, or a position where hard work and attention are requisite."

My great-great-grandfather George Dadson is pictured top left in the portrait that hangs in the Cranston Museum. Next to him are Amelia and his son George Dadson, my great-grandparents, Fred's mother and father and Dad's grandparents. Middle row, from left: Fred's sisters Edith and Ada, and baby Fred. Last row: At left is the Corsican that Fred travelled on in 1909. It was shipwrecked in 1923 near Cape Race, Newfoundland. These voyages to a new life were not without their risk. The final image is of the Dadson Bakery in England.

Chapter 14

Liverpool to Parry Sound

The Minnicoganashene, Penetang, Ontario
February 11, 1903
Dear Miss Leaman (sic),143 Ontario Street, Toronto
"You promised me to come back to me this year, and I am writing to find out if you will do so. I am not asking many to return… you were, in my opinion, one of the very few who knew how to do things suitable for the high class of people I have here… Yours truly, J. C. Cautley."

Lydia Leamen

The letter in this chapter from a Georgian Bay resort owner revealed the success that Lydia enjoyed in the work she pursued as a young, single woman. I imagined the day it arrived at her home in Toronto in 1903, six years before Fred arrived on the scene.

A cold February day, New Toronto, Ontario, 1903

"The mail is on the table Liddie - you have a letter." Lucretia called from the kitchen, using the familiar short form of her sister's name.

Lydia had just come through the front door after a day of work. Hanging her coat, scarf, and hat on the hall hook, she rubbed her arms against the cold. Lucretia was setting out a pot of tea for them as she entered the kitchen. Lydia picked up her nephew, Russell, gave him a kiss and a hug and then set him back down with his older brother Cecil to play.

"Thanks, Cretia (her nickname for her younger sibling). This is just what I need." Lydia poured a cup of tea. As her sister went about preparations for dinner, Lydia sat down to enjoy the hot drink and her letter.

After a fortifying sip, Lydia checked the postmark which showed it was from her boss at the resort on Georgian Bay where she worked last summer. She smiled at the boys playing at her feet, but at 26, she was able to make decisions for herself, an independence that came from not having a husband and children. As much as she loved her family, the job at the northern resort was an opportunity to live more independently, away from Lucretia and Walter. She loved the resort location on the water and availed herself of the opportunity to meet people from different places. She enjoyed the company of the other staff and embraced the work.

The typed letter from Mr. J.C. Cautley was flattering, and he was trying very hard to get her to return, promising improvements.

"I have engaged a very nice lady to take over entire charge, and I hope everything will be a great change for the better from last year and work very smoothly. The arrangements for the help's dining room will be greatly improved."

Perhaps securing unmarried young women to work was a challenge. Employers would need mature women, able to live away from home. Although the early part of the century saw opportunities for women change, many would still believe their choices in life were limited to domestic service or marriage.

Employers would not have considered married or pregnant women. It would be decades before opinions about working women evolved.

While we don't know when or why Lydia left Penetang, she did eventually find work in Parry Sound at The Belvidere. Perhaps it was better working conditions, and she could prove her value as an employee worth engaging with written recommendations, as noted above. Fred wrote his proposal on The Belvidere's letterhead and placed it in a resort envelope addressed only with the name: Lydia Leaman (sic). The assumption is that she was employed at The Belvidere.

Since Fred's proposal letter is undated, we can also only surmise when the offer of marriage happened. The best guess would be the summer of 1910, not long after Fred arrived in Canada. Their original marriage certificate, signed by Samuel W. Fallis, Pastor at Yonge Street Methodist Church, 37 Woodlawn Ave. W., Toronto, is dated September 7, 1910. It would appear the marriage followed immediately after the end of the summer season.

I can only imagine what caused this independent woman to take a chance on this relationship with an Englishman 12 years her senior.

Parry Sound, Ontario, circa summer 1910

Lydia looked out the dining-room window and watched Mr. Dadson, or Fred, as she now thought of him. He strolled along the wide veranda that wrapped around the hotel. He was not a large man, not much taller than her own five feet and six inches. While he walked, he smiled and tipped his black top hat at women he passed. Such a gentleman, she thought, and his English accent was a final touch to the image, she mused. He always spoke with precise attention to proper vocabulary and syntax.

As he came to a stop, examining the flowers planted along the porch, she recalled a recent conversation.

"I take delight in gardening," he told her. "At home, I experimented with grafting plants and attained some success." The gardens and walking trails at Belvidere were popular, and they attracted him to enjoy a holiday here. He had not been in Canada long. As he reflected on his next steps, she shared her lifelong knowledge of the Toronto area.

Over the summer, they had many conversations about gardening and other topics such as education, politics, and religion. She found him attentive and loved to hear about his life in England and his decision to come to Canada. He spoke of a cousin, a name she had heard in the Baptist tradition, *Rev. Ebeneezer Dadson. Fred listened to her when she expressed her opinions, and she appreciated this show of respect. She told him about her good friend Mae, who lived and worked in Detroit. He seemed to appreciate her maturity. When they observed younger women at the resort giggling and acting silly, he ignored them. She knew he had been married in England to an older woman who had died, and he had an adult son who lived in Ottawa.

As the subject of her musings rose, he looked toward the window. Bright grey eyes that sparkled within a darker, smoky grey rim captivated Lydia. The arresting gaze complemented a distinguished salt and pepper beard. She felt her heartbeat begin to race, and the sense her life was about to change overcame her.

"I'm acting like a schoolgirl, not a mature woman," she admonished herself.

She reflected again on his letter tucked in a drawer in her room. Is this the man she would trade her independent life for, the person with whom she would share her life?

While we don't know the exact timing and circumstances that brought my grandparents together, there are a couple of possibilities. Perhaps they met in Toronto, and Fred followed Lydia to Parry Sound. More likely is that Fred was in the resort area to connect with some cousins. An uncle, brother to his father George, had immigrated earlier and had a summer home in Muskoka on Cranbrook Lane. Perhaps Fred used some of Syd's inheritance to fund the courtship as a resort guest.

If every love story deserves some mystery, then Fred and Lydia left their share of unanswered questions; however, we know Lydia found a spot in her heart to accept Fred's proposal. The two created a home where they welcomed and loved three sons. No doubt she shared her own family story with Fred, which included both English and Irish ancestry, and her Canadian roots were deeper.

As I discover the musical score of their love story, I can hear Dad's soft notes in the dark floating back to me.

*Rev. Ebeneezer Dadson, son of Stephen and Mary (Breachin) Dadson, born in Cranbrook, Kent, England. Stephen was apparently a brother to my great-grandfather George. Thus, Ebeneezer would be a first cousin to Fred. The family came to Canada in 1849 settling in Toronto.

Chapter 15

Moonlight Serenade

March 23, 1944
My Dear Wife: … The Ink Spots are singing "Stormy Weather," and
I'm thinking of home… I love my wife. I love our baby Ricky, and oh,
how I miss them… Yours always, Murray.

Murray

Toronto, Circa 1966

It's dusk as we pull out of the driveway, tummies full after
Sunday dinner at Aunt Bette and Uncle Ray's. Mom drives and
Dad navigates.

We circle a ramp, and the car picks up speed on the 401. As
we leave the city lights behind, it gets darker in the car.

I crawl up to the shelf under the rear window and stretch out
on my back. One leg dangles onto the seat as support, and I
stare out the window at the night sky. I wonder if I can identify
the big or little dipper, or the north star. I try to remember what
Dad taught me from his navigator training.

The car is quiet. Now Dad sings.

"All day tomorrow, I'll be loving you and then, on the day after
forever, I'll start right in again." The mellow tones aka Bing

Crosby float from the front passenger seat.

"How about Paper Doll," I call. And he obliges.

"I'm going to buy a paper doll that I can call my own, a doll that other fellows cannot steal…"

I sing with him: "A doll that other gals cannot steal,"

Dad: "When I come home at night, why she'll be waiting. She'll be the truest doll in all the world,"

I sing: "When I come home at night, why he'll be waiting. He'll be the truest doll in all the world,"

Dad corrects me: "Slow down. You sing too fast."

He continues with his repertoire. My Blue Heaven *"… a cozy nook that's nestled where the roses bloom, there's just Molly and me, and the baby makes three…"* or Mona Lisa *"… men have named you…"* or Be Sure it's True *"… when you say I love you, it's a sin to tell a lie…"* or if my brothers are in the car, they call for The Whiffenpoof Song (1).

To the tables down at Mory's

To the place where Louie dwells

To the dear old Temple Bar we loved so well

Sing the Whiffenpoofs assembled with their glasses raised on high

And the magic of their singing casts its spell.

I could lie on the back shelf of the car forever, looking at the stars and listening to the magic as Dad casts his spell all the way home.

In music and in words, Dad openly shared his romantic view of life. He respected Mom. This was based on the deep respect he had for his own mother, described by some in the family as an angel.

(1). The Whiffenpoofs are an a Capella singing group out of Yale University, founded in 1909.

Chapter 16

Lydia Leamen

November 11, 1849
Dear Jemima (Lydia's grandmother): *I take this opportunity of sending you these few lines hoping to find you and the children in good health as this leaves me in at present. Thanks be to God for all his mercys. (Sic). I am now at present in New Orleans… do not be in the least uneasy about me for as soon as lies in my power I will send you as much as I can, and request of your father that he will take as much care of the children and you as lies in his power and I will make it all good to him… I remain your most affectionate husband untill (sic) death, Christopher Johnston.*

Lydia Jane Jemima Leamen

When my parents were dating, my mother sometimes stayed at the Dadson's, sleeping with Lydia on a pull-out couch in the living room. As Lydia talked about her family, my mother made polite responses while nodding off to sleep. And when Lydia brought her a cup of tea in the morning, my mother politely choked it down. She preferred coffee. In later years, she regretted not listening more carefully to Lydia's stories, being too young to appreciate the history being shared.

I know less about the Leamen side of the family tree, neither

Mom nor Dad being able to fill in the blanks. Lydia's grandfather wrote the letter featured in this chapter to her grandmother in 1849. It was postmarked UC (United Canadas as the British colony was called then). Thus, the family lived in Toronto prior to confederation. Difficult to read, the paper is stained with age, and there's a few missing lines because of rips. In addition, the penmanship is elaborate. We can discern that Christopher traveled to the U.S. and was in New Orleans, ostensibly looking for work. The address on the outside is Patrick McBrine in Toronto, likely Jemima's father and thus Lydia's great-grandfather. He is buried in Necropolis Cemetery, Toronto.

Some reading between the lines of what we know, along with some conjecture, can help to build a picture of Lydia, the woman who attracted Fred's attention and raised my father and his brothers. Everything that my father said about his mother points to a woman who loved her sons unconditionally, and who raised them with a wisdom that age and experience provided. Religion played a stronger role in her backstory.

Lydia Jane Jemima Leamen was born April 27, 1876, fourth child and first daughter to John Clement Leamen and Elizabeth (Keziah) Johnston in York, Ontario. (1) Her father was a Yardmaster for the Grand Trunk Railway, a founding member of Jones Avenue Baptist Church, and one of the oldest members of the Albion Lodge Sons of England. The family, including older brothers Christopher, Joseph, and Robert, lived at 293 Jones Avenue in Toronto. A younger sister, Lucretia, was born four years later to be followed by the sorrow of two infant deaths.

John Clement Leamen's newspaper obituary notes he was "well-known as Grandpa to the children of the Jones Avenue Baptist Church" and that among his effects was a Bible left to his son Robert.

Lydia was named, in part, for her maternal grandmother, Jemima Johnston, who in 1881 was living with Keziah and John and their five children. In addition, the census notes Jemimia (sic) was born in Ireland.

I was always curious about why my grandmother never married until she was 34, or what caused her to choose marriage then, and Dad could not enlighten me. I wondered - was she also very independent and remained single by choice, an idea I flirted with as a teenager? Did she turn down suitors before Fred in favour of the spinster life? Did Fred simply sweep her off her feet?

In my grandfather's trunk, which was in our family home, were two framed, formal portraits of my grandparents, the images taken before the two knew each other. I have studied her image over the years trying to glean something about this woman who my father adored, but whom I never knew. Taken possibly when she was in her early 20s, she had a symmetrical, oval-shaped face, intelligent light-coloured eyes, a slender nose, and a small mouth. A hint of a smile. Her thick brunette hair is swept loosely up on her head. An attractive woman, whom I imagine drew her share of potential suitors.

Her image reflects what those who knew her said, that she had a sweet disposition. "A saint," according to my brother Rick.

She pursued employment at vacation resorts during the summer months. These jobs exposed her to many people and required her to interact with vacationing guests. Moreover, her work ethic was such that an employer sought her out to return. That she pursued this employment for close to 10 years before marrying speaks to her character and suggests an affinity for something outside of the traditional in her life. Another picture of her, in later years, shows her standing in Lake Ontario, the water up to her knees. She is holding her dress up and out of the water. She clearly had a sense of fun about her, evident as well in the stories of her teen-aged boys teasing her.

When she met Fred in Parry Sound, she was past the years a woman expected to marry and raise a family-maybe another woman's motherless children, but to bear her own? Yet marriage seemed to agree with her. A family portrait taken in 1922 included her sons, their dog Prince, and Fred and Lydia, all standing in front of their home. Lydia, about age 45, still had a pretty, oval-shaped face, thinner than her younger portrait, her cheekbones more defined. She wound her hair in a braid on the back of her head. She had a clear, unlined complexion. An attractive woman and mother of three boys, the oldest of whom almost reached her height in the picture. Life, if appearances are any indication, was good. Dad's stories about his mother suggested a woman of faith who had a sense of humour and who valued friendship. And she seemed to have been a match for the older man who convinced her to say, "I do."

Exploring Lydia's father's history provided some details of relevance to Canadian history. Perhaps these were among the stories my mother missed while nodding off on that pull-out couch.

(1) I could not source any birth records for Kezia or Keziah or Elizabeth Johnston or Johnson, or marriage records for Jemima and Christopher Johnston or Johnson. Keziah's marriage record to John C. Leamen names her as Elizabeth Johnson and her parents only as Christopher and Jemima.

Lydia Leamen and Fred Dadson met at the Belvidere Resort in Parry Sound (below). Marriage followed. The above photos were taken before they met. Below, Lydia appears to be on a rock in Muskoka. The photo is not dated; she is younger with no grey hair, but her style of dress suggests it was taken after the time they met.

Chapter 17

Fenian Raids

The Irish American army boarded barges and crossed the Niagara River to undertake one of the most outlandish missions in military history — to kidnap the British colony of Canada, hold it hostage and ransom it for Ireland's independence. In fact, the self-proclaimed Irish Republican Army attacked Canada not just once, but five times between 1866 and 1871 in what are collectively known as the Fenian Raids. - (Klein, Time.com, 2019)

John Clement Leamen

My father was a very proud Canadian. Perhaps Lydia nurtured this because of her father's background. He played a minor role in the history pages of Confederation. That place in history was likely a point of pride for her.

John Leamen was a Fenian Raid Veteran. He fought against the Fenians, who wanted to secure Ireland's independence from Britain by holding Canada ransom. The movement involved a series of armed raids coming from the United States, taking place as Canada was planning to form a confederation. In light of this, some historians posit that these Fenian raids helped to shore support for the new confederation.

Records show that Lydia's father mustered as a Private with the Tenth Royal Grenadiers (now called the Royal Regiment of Canada) in June 1866 in Fort Erie. They discharged him the same year.

He may have been involved in the Battle of Ridgeway, which took place on the morning of June 2, 1866, near the village of Ridgeway when the Fenians crossed the border near Fort Erie. The battle, also known as the Battle of Lime Ridge, involved around "850 Canadian soldiers clashing with 750 to 800 Fenians. It was the last battle to be fought in Ontario against a foreign invasion force." (1) There were casualties in this war and the site was designated as a National Historic Site.

The Canada General Service Medal Register includes the name Private Leamen and the notation: "LaPrairie, Fort Erie and Thorold attack expected."

As we know, Confederation proceeded in 1867, and the following year on May 13, John married Keziah Johnston, a woman with Irish roots, when both were the age of 21.

This historical perspective of the Fenians is not something I recall Dad ever mentioned. Perhaps he didn't know about it. He said he knew little about his mother's family but believed they had deep Canadian roots. While Lydia's mother was born in Canada, maternal grandparents Jemima and Christopher were born in Ireland, and her father was born in Coffin's Wall, Torquay, England. The Canadian roots are not as deep as my mother's side as we will see.

While the Fenian cause was unsuccessful, perhaps its historical significance was lost in the major events of the following years, including two world wars and a depression.

Lydia was 21 when her mother died at age 50 in 1897. John Leamen married again in 1899 to Mary Ann Inward Sammon who died six years later. Then, in December 1910 he married his third wife, Minnie Nelson. John Clement Leamen passed away in 1918 at 72, so he lived to see the birth of Lydia's three sons.

Lydia's younger sister, Lucretia, married Walter Harris in 1900. The 1901 census notes Lydia lived with her sister and brother-in-law on Ontario Street. Part of the motivation to live with them may have been the presence of a new wife who also had three children. In addition, Lydia worked as a machine operator, although it is not noted where exactly. At this time in Toronto, many women found work in the garment industry, commercial bakeries, and book binderies as machine operators. It was better pay than domestic service, the only kind of work previously available to unmarried women in the working classes. Opportunities for unmarried women were expanding. (2)

Lydia's brothers also had their own families. She may have been close to her brother Joseph and his wife, Annie Elizabeth Mortimer. This couple had a son named Norman. Lydia later named her first child Clarence Mortimer and her second son Norman Murray. The youngest son Jack was named for her father John Clement.

However, my father's name, Murray, also honoured another significant relationship that Lydia maintained all her life. Getting to know Lydia requires a look into Mae Murray, the dear friend my father recalled his mother visiting in Detroit.

(1) Canadian Encyclopedia
(2) Gray, Charlotte, The Massey Murder A Maid, Her Master and the Trial that Shocked a Country.

Three brothers above left: Pete holds the rabbit while Murray sits, and Jack (Nink) stands behind him. Right: A young family in the home garden, Murray, Lydia, Jack, Pete with Prince, and Fred (c 1923).

Left: Fred and Lydia as grandparents, possibly with Rick (c 1941). Lydia with oldest son, Clarence (Uncle Pete).

Both Lydia and Fred brought a sense of fun to the marriage.

Chapter 18

A Treasured Friendship

5281 Vancouver Street, Detroit
Dec. 29, 1930
Dearest Lydia… Be of good cheer dear girl. I know you too have many
problems… Remember me kindly to Mr. Dadson and give Jack and
Murray a hug for me and tell Clarence that I send my love and best
wishes and if you will tell me the kind of books he likes, I'll send him
one from this side… Much love, Sincerely, Mae.

Mae Murray

When I was growing up, my father expressed the wish he could have just one more conversation with his parents. Now in my sixth decade, I can relate. I would love to chat with my parents, but if such a thing were possible, I would add my grandmother Lydia Dadson and her good friend Mae Murray to the request.

The friendship intrigues me because my research revealed that Mae was a spinster and the primary wage-earner in her home. Mae worked in a key administrative position for 47 years at a land development company, on a Grade 8 education. The 1940 United States Census lists Mae Murray as single, aged 64, head of the household, and born in Canada. Her brother George lived in the home and was 72. She earned $900 annually for a 40-hour week, 48 weeks of the year. (1)

The wages likely reflected what a woman earned, but Mae's employer appeared to reimburse her loyalty in different ways. He stopped her from handing out her own money to people during the depression. He provided tickets for food or a bed to hand out to people who showed up at the office everyday looking for work or handouts. In January 1939, she listed in a letter the Christmas gifts she received from friends, adding, "... *and last-but not least-a new Ford car from my employer so if I make Toronto or you come here, we will be riding in a 1939-very nice..."* In October of the same year, her boss gave her a trip to

New York to the World's Fair: *"Mr. Williams decided I needed a change for a few days as he said he would send me and his cousin Rose, who is one of my close friends, on the trip and the company would stand all expenses."* I could speculate on what these seemingly expensive gifts from her boss might have meant, but I decided to focus on the friendship instead.

< Mae Murray fishing at Grand Bend

This friendship with a working woman who remained single continued throughout Lydia's life. It wasn't unusual for Lydia to go to Detroit for a visit. I have combined details from Mae's letters, that span the depression through to the 50s, with Dad's memories, and a dose of my own imagination, to portray what these friends discussed on their visits.

Circa Summer 1931

"It is such a blessing to have this friendship last through all of life's changes," Lydia said, squeezing Mae's arm. The two women, friends since school days in Toronto, strolled arm in arm along Vancouver Street in Detroit, where Mae lived with her family.

"Oh, that is true, dear girl. I was listening to a radio program the other evening with music from our bygone days. I could hardly hold the tears back; it made me miss you and the others so much."

Lydia smiled. "I love listening to Enrico Caruso myself. His voice was beautiful."

The women strolled a few more feet, lost in memories, when Mae sighed.

"What's wrong?" Lydia prompted.

Mae smiled at her good friend's insight into her feelings. She nodded toward a home they were passing. "See that home over there? The family lost it. It makes my heart break to see so many up-and-doing families lose their homes.

"Some of these people were friends and the men just can't find work."

Lydia commiserated. "There is pain and suffering all over; I see it in Toronto too."

Mae expounded. "Business conditions are in a mess in Detroit. I do what I can, and Mr. Williams has allowed me to hand out tickets for meals, or a bed if needed. Our company has helped where it can, but the need is great."

Mae paused in reflection, then continued.

"You are fortunate, my good friend, that Mr. Dadson remains employed."

Lydia could see Mae's tiny, one-story home down the street. She reflected on Mae's need to keep working to support the house she shared with her older brother and their mother until her mother's death a year ago.

"Yes, we are fortunate," she echoed Mae's words. "Dominion has been good to us. Remember when Fred was ill, just after Murray was born? They continued to send us money to help meet our bills until Fred was back on his feet." (2)

Mae asked: "Do the boys help?"

"Yes, where they can," Lydia responded. "But Fred and I want them to finish school. I refuse to let them quit, like so many of their friends have done. We believe education will be important for their futures. I'm so glad Fred and I agree on this."

She thought about her busy home. Her three boys were becoming young men. Their pranks kept her on her toes, that was for sure, but she knew they were good young men, and she prayed every day for their futures. Right now, Murray and Jack were riding their bikes from Toronto up to Gravenhurst for a couple of weeks of camping with friends. She recalled the time a car hit Murray on his bike. Thank God he was okay. No broken bones. Now she worried when they travelled such a distance. She had other concerns as well.

"I worry about the boys' futures. So many young men are leaving Toronto to find work. I need to keep them at home," she gave voice to her motherly worries.

Mae stopped and turned to her friend. "Well, they will leave someday Lydia. But at least you and Mr. Dadson will have each other." Then, as she continued to walk on, she added, "Here is a thought. I see our neighbour's boy tinkering on his car all day.

Would you be able to find a used car that needs work-something to keep them occupied?"

Lydia laughed. "What a wonderful idea. I will have to check into that."

The women continued their walk, enjoying the cooler evening air.

As they got closer to Mae's home, Lydia said, "I admire you, Mae, and what you have accomplished. You have been successful at William's."

Mae shook her head. "I'm not so sure I have accomplished all that much. I had such dreams, but my days, Lydia, are so full. I work, come home, do the shopping and cooking, and then I'm exhausted.

"Yes, I had dreams, but you know my story. If it weren't for gin and whiskey, I would not be compelled to turn out each and every day to make a living and support a home."

Lydia thought about her own situation and Fred's brewing of his own beer at home. The man did like his drink.

"Yes, the drinking worries me as well. I don't understand men sometimes, even though I now live in a house full of them."

Mae chuckled. "Yes, they have their weaknesses. George can be difficult at times, but I must admit, I have come a long way about not saying too much to him about it. He does like to have a few drinks for himself, and I just know he has to do that, and if he gets any pleasure out of it, well-it just is all right with me."

Alcohol seemed to be a topic of concern for both women. I don't know Mae's full story or what she meant when she blamed alcohol for her situation in one of her letters. Was it her father, whom she never mentions?

My grandfather liked his drink. A letter from the Department of Customs and Excise, Ottawa, dated October 1922, notes his proposal of "brewing beer for your own use" and cautions him there would be a penalty if he sold the beer. He didn't sell it, and I recall Dad saying something about drinking his dad's beer.

It was not unusual for Lydia to send granddaughter Joyce to get Fred out of the hotel to come home for dinner. However, it was a police escort that brought him home on one occasion. I grew up with the story that this happened in his late 80s; my cousin Wendy added some context to the story. Apparently, there was a younger man in the bar who was swearing. Fred took offence by striking him with his cane! Police were called, and they brought Fred home. Defender of proper English language. He would be aghast if he heard the language on any university campus today.

Dad recalled arriving to take his father out for a beer but being told by Fred that he had quit drinking alcohol. This happened around age 90, and he died at 94.

While the stories of drinking were part of the history about the grandfather I never knew, alcohol wasn't a controlling factor in our family. Both of my parents drank alcohol, but they didn't abuse it; instead, it was part of the social fabric when friends or family gathered, a cold beer on the front porch or while they watched the soaps, the news, or a hockey game on TV; they served wine and liqueurs at family dinners.

Rather, I think if there was a legacy left by Fred and Lydia, it was in the love and respect they showed each other. Lydia's friendship with Mae is a part of that picture. It remains true that "as women's obligations to family life increase, their friendships tend to suffer or disappear altogether." (3) Despite being separated by several hours' train ride across a border, these women sustained their connection (without social media) throughout Lydia's marriage and supported it with in-person visits over the years.

Dad recalled that around his 16th birthday, he rode his bicycle from Toronto to Gravenhurst. With Frank Camry, Bill Cassman, and Nink, they took three days to get there, with a home-made trailer attached to one bike. They spent two weeks camping before returning home, 120 miles, in one day. Dad said he was homesick, but when he arrived home, his mother was not there. It was a cause for concern, but he laughed at the memory. She had just travelled to Detroit to visit her good friend, Mae Murray.

The friendship continued as the family matured. A reference to my parents in August 1950 is amusing: *"Of course Murray passed whatever course he tried, and I am not at all surprised that he is "going places." Glad they have a nice car, and that*

Ginger is going to sit in the driver's seat - once in a while - ha ha."

< Ginger at the wheel likely in Jack's car!

While it might be too much to suggest Fred was a modern man to allow the women's friendship to flourish, I think it deeply shows his respect for her and his desire to foster her happiness.

Like Murray tried to foster Ginger's. It was a challenging task as he was fighting demons that he didn't know about because of a story Mom and her sisters kept to themselves.

(1) That $900 in 1940 would equal just over $17,000.00 in 2020 so not a huge annual salary. Women's wages? Unskilled or uneducated labour rates? Consider that 20 years before this in 1921, my maternal grandfather was earning $2,000 as a foreman in an auto store in the Windsor area.

(2) A letter signed by James Tom on Dominion Paper Box Company letterhead Dec. 13, 1916, "Dear Fred: You will find enclosed 25.00 dollars which I hope will keep you going for a little while, & I will see that more will come up to you, don't worry, but get better & do not come out too soon or you may get a relapse. Hoping you have a speedy recovery." This support continued the rest of the month to help the family through Christmas. While the nature of the ailment is not specified, I wonder if it was eczema.

(3) New York Times book review by Ann Friedman on "The Social Sex: A History of Female Friendship" by Marilyn Yalom and Theresa Donovan Brown notes: "Godey's Lady's Book," a popular women's journal in 19th-century America, reflected social mores at the time in extolling the bonds between women as paramount—until a husband entered the picture.

Chapter 19

Secrets

March 14, 1944
…Don't ever write to me again and ask me whether I have forgotten
you and Rick. I have so many fond memories and think so damn much
of my family that it would be impossible to forget. Write again soon,
Sweetheart. Good night and kisses to you both.

Sharon

The war separated families and tested newlyweds, as this
chapter's letter suggests. While some of Dad's letters addressed
Mom's insecurities, I wonder if he truly understood how much
she needed his constant declarations of love.

After the war, Dad's commitment to Campbell Soup paid off
in promotions and better pay, and the family moved in 1953
from crowded Fourth Street to a new subdivision in Toronto.
And Sharon, the only daughter of Mom's sister Bette, came to
live with them. When I asked about this history, Mom's
explanation satisfied my innocent curiosity: "Aunt Bette was
divorced and dating. We thought it inappropriate for a young
girl to be at home when her mother was dating."

The truth was much uglier.

I didn't learn about it until around 1980, early in my marriage. I was outside when a car stopped in front of the house. My cousin Sharon, about 12 years my senior, walked up the driveway. She was direct and to the point.

"I want to let you know that John and I have separated. There's something else. You should know, our grandfather, our mothers' father, sexually abused me when I was a child."

Stunned by Sharon's words, tears threatened as I tried to absorb her news.

Shock. Shame. Embarrassment. I felt sick to my stomach.

Unsure of what to do with the emotions or the information, I did not respond in the best way possible. I believed Sharon, had no reason to doubt her, but I didn't offer any comfort.

Much later, I spoke to Sharon. I spent a lot of time reflecting on the ramifications, for Sharon, but also for our mothers. We agreed, it is unlikely that Sharon was his first victim. That knowledge explained my immediate reaction to her news. I knew, on some level, this was an important piece of information about Mom. Regrettably, I never spoke to my mother about it. How do you ask your mother-did your father sexually abuse you? Maybe I didn't want to know the answer. Denial can serve as a refuge.

Sharon was only about 4 or 5 years of age when the molestation happened. Our grandparents, Nanie and Pop, lived with her along with her mom, my Aunt Bette, and our Aunt Peg. My mother's sisters. Sharon had laid down for a nap, and Pop joined her. Aunt Peg came home, and when she learned that Pop was napping with Sharon, she entered the room.

Sharon's memories, some in the form of smell, came at the expense of many visits to psychiatrists, therapy sessions, and a failed marriage. In the immediate aftermath of the discovered abuse, Sharon was sent to live with an uncle and aunt, a brother of her father's. Then she went to her father's, an arrangement that lasted for about five years until he and his second wife divorced.

Sharon was visiting my parents when her mom telephoned. She told Sharon to call her dad from Uncle Murray and Aunt Ginger's and tell him she was now living with them.

"It's the first time I felt part of a real family," Sharon said about living with her aunt and uncle. She helped to feed Miles, who was a baby, and she and Rick became close friends. He was like an older brother; in fact, he traveled back from Rutgers University a few years later to escort Sharon to her high school graduation. She recounted she had difficulty connecting with boys.

However, what felt like an ideal family arrangement didn't last. When Dad received a transfer to the United States, he didn't think it was fair to take Sharon so far from her parents. Years later, Sharon told my father she was devastated by the split. He was remorseful. Had he known, he would have taken her too, he said. This conversation took place long before Sharon revealed the abuse to me. Dad never knew.

The implication that we can't verify is whether Mom and her sisters were also molested. Research would suggest that a grandfather who abused a granddaughter probably has a history of abuse. It leaves us with many questions.

Did Aunt Peg walk in on Sharon and Pop because she knew something was wrong due to her own experience?

Was Aunt Peg's youthful marriage at 17 an attempt to get out of the house?

Did Mom's lack of recall about her childhood protect her from memories too painful to recall?

Was Mom a victim, or did one or both of her sisters protect her?

Was Mom's anger at her mother because she ignored what happened?

How did this secret stalk my mother into her marriage?

As an adult, Sharon asked her mom why she was sent away. They had consulted a lawyer, she was told, who advised them to remove the child immediately. They took no action against the perpetrator. If it had gone to court, Sharon would have to testify in front of her grandfather. It's how the legal system treated children in those days. Sharon tried to speak to my mother, but Mom would not discuss it with her.

I just can't imagine that my father knew about it. If Mom thought news would upset him, she would keep information from Dad. She did it with us kids. Dad had a temper. She likely thought, or knew, this would be too much for him to handle. Talking about the intimate aspects of life was not done casually or easily in our household. Surely, Dad would never have allowed Sharon to be returned to the same house as her grandfather had he known. Because that is what eventually happened.

Sharon shakes her head about that. First, she was returned to live with her mom. Then they lived with Aunt Peggy in an apartment. Finally, the grandparents joined them. While no more abuse happened, it could be said that many of the adults in her life failed Sharon.

This story casts a shadow on what we know of Mom's family. What would further research into this side of the family reveal?

Murray in his air force uniform, holding son Rick with Ginger at his side. Marriage and war brought more responsibilities. Ginger is pictured as a working mother (picture of Rick on the mantle). Murray in his navigator's seat on a plane (looking very much like son Bill). The Ruthven Sisters, as Dad called them, like a unit. A unit with secrets, perhaps.

Chapter 20

The Blank

April 4, 1944
My Darling Ginger: ... I haven't told you yet Hon, but I love you.
Every time I come back from a forty-eight, I go around in a daze. Even
when I close my eyes, I see you. It's just Ginger - Ginger - Ginger. It
takes a couple days before I can get back in the groove... Goodnight
Darling, Murray.

The Ruthvens

Mom said little about her youth; the specific phrase she used when describing her life to me was "it is like a fog-I don't remember anything."

She had four siblings, two sisters and two brothers. She remained close to sisters Peggy and Bette, and when she could see him, her brother Larry. We rarely saw her brother Bus.

Mom's sister Peggy, the eldest of the family, was a favourite of ours, likely because she didn't have children of her own and doted on us. Jan and Bill both stayed with Aunt Peg when they worked summer jobs in Toronto. A high school friend and I stayed with her after a day at the CNE. Cousin Sharon spent a good deal of her youth living with Aunt Peg.

Peggy married Francis (Frank) Jones in 1931 when she was just 17. Their divorce was finalized in 1951, but the marriage didn't last anywhere near that long. Mom told me that her sister was in the hospital because of a miscarriage when her husband showed up in uniform to tell her he was leaving her.

Photos of the three sisters show three beautiful young women, but it was Aunt Peg who really stood out. A photographer approached her once about modelling, but her mother forbade it. Aunt Peg supported herself working at Campbell Soup in Toronto, where she oversaw the mailing department. Attractive, she had her share of attention from men, including the man who stood her up in Montreal when Peg showed up at Mom and Dad's hotel room. Alluded to but never discussed openly was that at least one of the relationships was with a married man; Sharon recalled one man who gave her and a girlfriend money to go get ice cream while he visited, effectively getting them out of the house. I speculate whether the possibility of abuse in Aunt Peg's youth contributed to her relationship troubles.

In later years Aunt Peg took up golf and enjoyed travel with friends. We all mourned her painful death from cancer in 1999 at 84.

< *Aunt Peg, Aunt Bette, and Mom c1970s*

Bette, the second oldest, waited until she was 27 before marrying Johnny O'Donovan in 1942, and they had Sharon the next year. The marriage lasted 15 months, but it was 15 years before the divorce was finalized. This paved the way for her to marry Raymond Yuill in 1957. Ray was part-owner with his brothers in a successful trucking firm, Yuill Cartage in Etobicoke.

In the early years, Aunt Bette and Uncle Ray lived in the same building as Aunt Peg on Macdonald Street, not far off Royal York Road in Mimico. Eventually, they moved to a large, four-bedroom home in a new area of Mississauga, but my aunt remained frugal. As a child of the depression, Aunt Bette painted her kitchen table rather than purchase a new one. She was embarrassed about the new chesterfield and lamps in her living room. She and Uncle Ray were walking in front of a store, and she commented she liked the suite in the window. Ray went in and bought the complete set.

This extravagance is noteworthy in an era when possessions were cared for and not easily replaced. For example, my parents had the same chesterfield they bought for their first home when they moved to Listowel some 25 years later. It became my first couch in my first apartment.

Uncle Ray drank enough that the beer truck delivered to their home. He slept until noon most days; in later years, he only went into work to sign pay cheques. Then, suddenly, he stopped drinking. He returned from a doctor's appointment one day and never drank again. He never revealed what prompted the change, and Aunt Bette told us the difference in him was astonishing. One morning, she burned part of his breakfast and fretted about it. He told her not to worry. In the past, he would have thrown the plate at her. We were glad for whatever had frightened him into sobriety. We discovered an uncle that enjoyed our company, and we enjoyed his in return.

This change also gave my aunt some good years before she died of cancer in 1985 at 70. Mom spent a lot of time at Bette's side during the illness and was with her when she died. It was an experience that shook her profoundly and made her adamant about keeping Dad in the hospital when he was dying.

Mom's brother Frederick was the oldest male and apparently a favoured son. He went by the name Bus or Buster and was married to Stella, with whom he had a son, Tony, a cousin I have never met. His second wife was Isabelle.

Just before she died, Mom had a visit from Bus, arranged by his stepdaughter. Mom could not talk because of her illness, but a pleasant visit occupied one afternoon. After he left, I wondered how she felt about seeing him. She wrote on her whiteboard, "After all, he is my brother." This brother died in 1999, a year after mom.

The youngest of the family, Larry, was epileptic, according to my mother, because the nurse held her mother's legs together at his birth, waiting for the doctor to arrive. Larry tried to enlist in the RCAF, but he was too young, so he went to England, lied about his age, and signed up with the RAF where he spent the war as a tail gunner. He never had seizures during the war. He married in Brussels, Belgium, in 1945 and returned home with his war bride, Giselle. They eventually moved to Arizona because their daughter suffered from asthma. He had two children, Linda and Larry, two more first cousins I never met. Uncle Larry and Giselle divorced, and in later years, he lived in California with a new partner, Sally. My parents visited them following Dad's retirement.

My only memory of Uncle Larry is a visit he made when I was around 20. Jim and I took my parents and Larry to the Queen's Hotel in Wellesley where the regular Saturday night entertainment was "Sing Along with Ferd." He played piano and sang all the old songs from my parents' time. On this night, Jim was the designated driver, and Mom and I sat in the front helping him drive home through a blinding rainstorm. In the backseat, Dad and his brother-in-law continued singing and called for "James" to take them home. There was real affection between the two. Larry died in 2007.

My mother's side of the family included many divorces. She was the only one of her siblings to remain married to the same person. It prompted a lot of my questions to her when I was young.

These were the children of Frederick Hugh Ruthven and Jessie Mary Chalmers. If Murray's parents, Fred and Lydia, provided a loving foundation that he carried into his life with Ginger, Fred and Jessie Ruthven's story provides insight into why Murray's confidence and love were a firm anchor in Ginger's life.

Chapter 21

A Difficult Beginning

March 14, 1944
... Hon. I love you, you will never understand how much. I miss our
little Rickey, too. Keep your chin up Sweetheart, remember you'll have
to be a mother and a father to him until I come home again. When you
read this, please smile for me, and say to yourself, "everything is
alright. Murray is still crazy about me and thinks of us always..."

Fred and Jessie (Chalmers) Ruthven

My maternal grandparents began married life under a cloud.
First, Fred's parents disowned him when he married a pregnant
Jessie. Then, a few short months later, their baby boy died.

This depressing start may have tainted the couple's life
together. Neither seemed able to face what life brought their
way, and alcohol served as an escape.

"He was born with a silver spoon in his mouth," Mom said of
her father, inferring that his family's money and stature didn't
prepare him for the real world. News articles confirmed the
family enjoyed some prominence in their community. Fred's
grandfather Hugh was namesake for the community of Ruthven
where he owned land and was an industrious businessman in

the area. Fred's father, Adolphus, was a well-known musician and businessman in Windsor.

In the 1911 census, Fred was 26 and living at the King George Hotel, as were his parents who owned the Hotel. The census listed Fred as a Clerk working at Engineering and earning $1,000 annually.

A couple of years later in March 1913, 28-year-old Fred married Jessie who was 21.

Unlike the Dadson's, who opened their home to sons and wives in the early years of marriage, the Ruthven's did not invite Fred and Jessie to make a home in the family hotel.

Jack Chalmers Ruthven was born in May, two months after the marriage. His death followed six months later in October. The death certificate listed the cause of death as marasmus, a form of severe malnutrition.

With the advantage of seeing into Fred and Jessie's future, it's possible to speculate that a case of misdiagnosed celiac caused the untimely death. Forty years later, in the early 1950s, doctors diagnosed my brother Miles with celiac, a hereditary digestive disease. He was six months old and unable to sit in his highchair. When left untreated, celiac can cause a condition in which the body cannot absorb nutrition from food. My brother ended up in Sick Kid's Hospital "on the verge of rickets and scurvy," my mother said.

A sister of Fred's, Emily Maud, also died at six months with the cause of death listed as catarrhal enteritis. Enteritis is an illness involving the intestines, causing digestion issues.

Is there a hereditary ailment involved? Is it possible Jessie and Fred's first baby, and Fred's sister, both had undiagnosed celiac?

Records show Jessie and Fred crossed into Detroit in 1914 with their daughter Margaret (Peggy) who arrived almost exactly one year, May 3, after Jack. I wonder at the fears my grandmother must have felt, knowing she carried another baby in her womb when Jack died. Then, one year later, Elizabeth (Bette) arrived in April 1915. Another trip into Detroit was recorded with the two daughters.

In two short years, Fred and Jessie married, anticipated three births, buried a son, and added two baby daughters to their home, and all while moving back and forth across the border. The instability of the changes in such a short time must have created a lot of stress.

And life continued to be difficult. Unlike Fred Dadson, who worked throughout the 1920s and the depression years, it appears Fred Ruthven had a hard time keeping jobs, and he moved his family frequently.

In 1918, a World War I draft registration card showed Fred and Jessie were living at 428 Cortland Ave., Detroit, Michigan. It listed him as an assistant foreman with the Ford Motor Company. In the same year, another son, Frederick Hugh (Bus), arrived. Given the death of Jack, this son may have been cause for celebration and why he appeared to be favoured by his mother. Then one year later, in August 1919, Virginia Carol (Ginger) was born. Their birth records show the family was living in Royal Oak, Michigan, a short distance from Detroit.

The couple now had four children under the age of five. In 1921, the family returned to Windsor and rented a row home on Chatham Street. Fred worked as a foreman in an auto store, earning a yearly salary of $2,000. At this time, Jessie's 63-year-old mother came to live with the family. This is one memory my mother did recall with fondness, that she was "basically raised" by her maternal grandmother. "We all loved her very much." She also said that her mother spent a year in a sanatorium for tuberculosis, but when that happened isn't clear. The grandmother's presence no doubt helped during the illness, and when Lawrence (Larry), affectionately called "Baby Larry" as the youngest of the family, was born in Windsor in 1922.

The apparent job success between 1918 and 1921 was followed in 1922 with Fred crossing back to Detroit on his own, perhaps to look for work. He was 37 and had five children to support.

I don't know exactly when it happened, or what prompted the move, but eight years later, in 1930, the family lived in Toronto. Fred was in Charlotte, Florida, working as an auto mechanic. This work lasted about a year before he returned to Canada.

Alcohol remained a problem. In one incident, my grandmother tripped, after drinking, over a small wire fence in the yard. The fall resulted in permanent damage to the tendons in her hand. Her left hand froze into a claw-like position, all four fingers and thumb bent inward at the knuckles.

"She never bothered to do the exercises the doctor gave her," Mom said without sympathy.

My mother said her parents frequently crossed the border while they lived in Windsor and that her mother even had a special vest made for transporting liquor. While prohibition ended in Canada at the end of the first world war, it continued in the United States until 1933, during years when the Ruthven family lived in Detroit.

When Peggy was 16, she got her father a job as a guard at the Campbell Soup plant after he returned from Florida. Shortly after this she left home to marry.

Mom's eventual marriage, the arrival of children, and multiple job transfers created distance between herself and her family. Although we visited our grandparents and her sisters when we moved closer to Toronto, I suspect the distance from family was desirable. When I consider what may have happened in her home, I can see more clearly what Murray meant for Ginger.

In addition, Dad's high school education, not something everyone in their circle achieved in those years, suggested a good future. Mom described herself as "stupid" and was ashamed that she never went past Grade 8. I always felt she would have excelled in business, and that she was wrong about herself. She had good instincts about people and tons of common sense, kept abreast of news, and managed the household budget like it was her business. But she would not be convinced.

She took a part-time job when I was in high school, approaching her salesclerk position at Stedman's professionally. She engaged with customers and essentially managed the place. This worked out well for the mostly absentee owner, until a younger man, related to the owner, came in to take over. You can imagine the rest. The most vulnerable I ever saw her was the day I dropped into the store on my way home from high school. Mom and her new boss were walking up the aisle, and both passed me. She looked stunned and didn't see me, didn't acknowledge me. Her young boss appeared upset to see me, and I went home stressed. The only thing I could think that would cause her to look like that would be Dad's death. She never spoke in anger about what happened, but in retrospect, the firing was clearly another blow to her confidence.

In later years, Jessie and Fred retired to Niagara-on-the-Lake. They lived in a one-bedroom apartment on the main level of a majestic, older home. An iron fence enclosed the expansive lot of gardens and trees that surrounded the house. They fed birds and squirrels at their kitchen window.

I was 10 when Pops died in 1966. I barely knew him. Nanie moved back to Toronto to live with Aunt Peg in her two-bedroom apartment. It was an unholy alliance fraught with frustration for my aunt. My grandmother was a bitter old lady.

Eventually, the sisters moved Nanie into a nursing home.

Many of the residents experienced different forms and levels of dementia. On visits, Dad would sing old tunes and soon many would join in, remembering the words. No doubt his visits were a highlight.

< Mom and Nanie in nursing home visit.

My grandmother died in 1976 when my parents were on their first-ever vacation to a southern island. They cut the trip short to return home, my mother taking on the guilt of having been away.

I continued to research the Ruthven history, curious about the backgrounds of both Fred and Jessie. I uncovered much more about my mother's ancestors, unknown to me, or my mother.

Chapter 22

The Bandmaster

March 23, 1944
*My Dear Wife: ... don't go tiring yourself out cleaning up the house
just before I come home. Just leave it, Hon, and I'll fix it up for you. I
mean that now... Yours always, Murray.*

Adolphus and Elizabeth (Chater) Ruthven

Fred Ruthven was the first, and only surviving, child of
Adolphus Ruthven and Elizabeth Nettie Chater. He arrived to the
name of Frederick Hugh, August 24, 1884, in Windsor. His
parents named him after an uncle on his mother's side and his
paternal grandfather, Hugh. A sister, Emily, was born and died
two years later.

The family background revealed a musical lineage that can be
traced back to my great-great-great-grandfather, Neil Ruthven,
who brought a violin to Canada when he left Scotland. The
violin eventually found its way to Adolphus who showed musical
talent from a young age. He taught music in Detroit for four
years prior to his marriage. Adolphus and Elizabeth married in a
Christmas eve ceremony in 1882, the same year that the groom
was given a clerkship in the Windsor post office. Adolphus was

26, and Elizabeth was 18, a daughter of Thomas Chater and Anne Maria Bull Chater. Her parents were both born in England and came to Windsor from New York in 1853. Their daughter and her five siblings were born in Windsor.

The post office position offered security to a married man, although Adolphus never gave up music. His talents gained notoriety in later years when he served as bandmaster of the 21st Regimental Band. In September 1904, they were the only Canadian band invited to the military ceremonies at the World Fair in St. Louis. The band also performed in Chicago on the same trip.

Fred H. Ruthven was a member of the 21st Regiment, Essex Fusiliers, in 1905, when Fred was 20. While it is no doubt my grandfather, I can't verify it. I never knew him to be musical; my mother never mentioned it.

Adolphus also had entrepreneurial instincts, purchasing the Iroquois Hotel from Thomas H. Bastle in late 1909. He renamed it King George a year later, after the coronation of King George following the death of King Edward VII. The hotel was not large, only three stories high, on the corner of Sandwich Street East and Goyeau Street, opposite the CNR Station. The family lived in the hotel.

Adolphus and Elizabeth combined business with their Scottish heritage when they hosted the local St. Andrew Society in 1910.

The Windsor Star featured a story about the celebration in its December 1 edition, noting: "Much credit is due Mr. and Mrs. Ruthven, of the King George Hotel, for the excellent repast. The cooking smacked of 'home,' and many compliments were bestowed on the host and hostess for their big share in making the event a success."

The St. Andrew Society is a social club focused on celebrating

Scottish tradition. It is named for the country's patron saint, Andrew, one of Christ's disciples. St. Andrew Societies are in many cities wherever Scottish immigrants settled. The news article allowed me to imagine one late November evening in which my great-grandparents celebrated the procession of the haggis with friends and associates:

Wednesday, Nov. 30, 1910

The loud, distinct call of bagpipes fill the room, and the buzz of guests greeting each other subsides in anticipation. Lights blaze overhead, jewellery sparkles on ladies' necks, and clan tartans add splashes of colour throughout the room. The men stand proud in kilts of bright shades of red, deep greens and brilliant blues, mixed with yellows and oranges, honouring the families and clans present.

Instinctively, Elizabeth's hand checks the sash of Ruthven tartan that runs over the shoulder of her deep blue tailored jacket. She likes the effect of the dominant red and blue with a small square of green at the centre against her matching jacket and skirt, purchased for this important evening.

Guests smile, nodding their heads and tapping their toes to the familiar strains of the piper. Elizabeth holds her chin high, casting a careful eye over the assembly and the proceedings. The arrival of the haggis is an important tradition and focus of celebrations on St. Andrew's Day, held annually on this date.

Elizabeth allows herself some satisfaction in their decision to host this event at the hotel. Over 100 distinguished guests from the business and social elite of Windsor fill the room. Some men, like Dr. G.R. Cruickshank, wear kilts. As president of the local St. Andrew Society, the doctor sits in the centre of the head table, the Royal Standard, representing the United Kingdom, draped behind him. Next to it is the bright blue and white cross of St.

Andrew. Around the room staff had placed additional flags, the Canadian Red Ensign, and the Union Jack, to add to the festive and patriotic nature of the event. Sitting on either side of the president are several of the Society's ex-presidents: James Kenning, George Bartlett, Dr. J.A. Smith, and James McSween.

Elizabeth watches as Adolphus approaches her, giving a small shake of his head. He'd left momentarily to look for their son. Elizabeth does her best to hide her disappointment. Frederick is missing an opportunity tonight to make some important connections in the city. His parents are anxious that he make a good match in marriage.

The stirring pipe music distracts the couple from their personal concerns. They watch the procession, which starts in the kitchen with George Nairn carrying the haggis; next in line are William Riddle, Stewart Murray, and Alex Moir. Waiters circulate the room pouring wine and the requisite whiskey and bring food to the tables. Besides haggis, other popular dishes include Scottish bannock, a spongy, buttery, raisin-filled cake; cock-a-leekie soup, a rich stew with chicken, leeks and rice; and beef and lamb stovies, a mix of potatoes, meat, and vegetables.

As people eat, the room quiets somewhat and Miss Moir and Mrs. George MacDonald sing, followed by soloist Duncan McMillan. The stirring tunes invoke memories of home and cause some eyes to glisten with tears. The crowd continues to be both entertained and called to express pride as a series of toasts, including many Scotch stories, are told with humour in between the musical numbers.

W. J. Black is exuberant in his toast to Canada: "The twentieth century belongs to Canada," he boasts. "Prosperity dwells in our vast country from ocean to ocean. The great northwest contains a wealth of land for the good man, and the Dominion is indeed a *country of opportunity."*

Elizabeth agrees with him about opportunities being plentiful and takes a few moments to appreciate what she and Adolphus have built in this community. Her husband began as an accountant in charge of the money order and savings bank department at the post office. His reputation as a musician continues to grow after his regimental band travelled to the World Fair in the U.S. Then, he saw an opportunity in this hotel and made a bold move. The change in name from Iroquois to King George enhanced its prominence in the city, and tonight is a culmination of that dream. Disappointment and anger floods her again as she thinks of her missing son.

She casts a protective eye toward her husband, who is in animated conversation with a group of businessmen. Of average height, he is slim and sports an impressive full moustache. He looks well tonight, but she knows his health is failing in small ways. Just old age, she thinks, but he needs to slow down a bit. Between the hotel and his band, the man is always busy.

One year after this event, in September 1911, The Windsor Star reported Adolphus was considering an offer to be chief bandsman on His Majesty's Ship, Niobe. The Niobe was one of two ships given to the Dominion of Canada to seed its new Canadian navy. The article quotes Adolphus as saying his health was not good, and that he was contemplating the sale of the hotel.

His death came five years later in 1916; more severe illness marked the last three years of his life. They listed the cause of death as arterio sclerosis (a hardening of arteries), "with insular sclerosis" or multiple sclerosis. He was 60 years old. This news about his health is noteworthy, as my mother had amyotrophic lateral sclerosis and one of Rick's daughters has multiple sclerosis.

An Essex Free Press news article about his passing noted his reputation as a musician. It included the detail that Adolphus possessed a 200-year-old violin that belonged to his grandfather, Neil Ruthven. There is no mention of daughter-in-law Jessie, or grandchildren, despite the fact Fred and Jessie were married for three years and had children.

His widow, Elizabeth, remarried two years later to a William Sinclair Treble. They lived in London, Ontario, for a while before William died in 1924 in Windsor. At some point Elizabeth moved to Toronto where she died at age 72. It isn't clear who moved to Toronto first, if Elizabeth followed her only son, or if Fred and Jessie followed Elizabeth. Elizabeth maintained some connection to her son's family as on her death in 1936, her estate was willed to Peggy and Bette. She left everything, valued at $10,000, to be divided between them. She effectively bypassed her son and left the estate to the oldest two granddaughters.

"Disowned and disinherited," in my mother's words. Perhaps this explains why Peg and Bette housed their parents at different times over the years, feeling obliged to step in because of the inheritance.

Considering the Scottish traditions supported by Elizabeth and Adolphus, and Fred's strained relationship with them, I'm left to wonder how my mother assimilated her Scottish roots with limited links to this past.

Top left, Adolphus Ruthven, possibly in his bandmaster's uniform, in the only photo I have of an ancestor of Mom's. Fred and Jessie Ruthven are beside a picture of their children. Peg is front and centre, flanked by Bette and Larry. A young Ginger stands next to Bus. Middle row: Aunt Peg (in a photo I always thought made her look like a Breck girl from the famous advertising campaign), Aunt Bette, and Mom (about age 17). In the bottom row Bus, then Larry in uniform beside an older image of Fred and Jessie with a cat.

Chapter 23

Traditions and Folklore

April 18, 1944
My Darling: This is my first letter in three days, and I am ashamed of myself; but as an excuse, I must say I have been kept busy. We were flying last night, and the night before, and in between there have been classes, and the exams are right upon us. I love you. Murray.

Ginger

Whether my mother just didn't know or didn't recall much of her family's past, she clearly absorbed and brought some customs into our home that are Scottish. For instance, First Foot suggests a dark-haired male should be the first to cross your threshold in a new year as a harbinger of good luck for the coming year. After my marriage to Jim, my mother asked him to come in the rarely used front door on New Year's Day, saying it was for good luck.

Her superstitious nature carried into other habits, including the lighting of bayberry candles every Christmas. The bayberry candle may have its roots in early American custom when the animal fat from slaughtered animals was used to make candles. Richer families used beeswax or bayberry wax for a better scent.

Bayberry, or wax myrtle, was made by boiling bushels of bayberries until the waxy substance seeped out of the berries; it involved a lot of extra work. As a result, they saved the candles for special times, such as Christmas. The legend began: "A bayberry candle burnt to the socket brings food to the larder and gold to the pocket." (1) Perhaps the Scottish family that made its way north from the U.S. brought the custom with them.

My mother always lit a bayberry candle on Christmas eve, Christmas night, and New Year's Eve. I guess she was covering all the bases. The candle had to be what she considered "real" bayberry, not just an artificial scent, and usually Bill or Jan was tasked with finding the correct ones in Toronto. She really wasn't taking any chances. She also said the candle could not be lit until dusk, and it must burn out on its own. Not understanding this aspect of the tradition, I lit a bayberry before dark one year, and she rushed to blow it out and cut the burned wick off. We went to bed many nights with the bayberry candle still burning, moved to a tin pie plate, and placed on top of the stove for safety.

One of the comfort meals she served at home was essentially a hamburger soup over mashed potatoes, called mince and tatties in Scotland.

Our home was a blend of English and Scottish traditions, including a more formal, polite approach to conversation, remembering to say please and thank you, calling our elders by their surnames, and respecting personal space. Dad was more likely to hug, but a stiff upper lip was expected, and tears were not tolerated. With friends they knew well, both Mom and Dad could be relaxed and affectionate.

Mom always wanted to add what she perceived to be a touch

of class to anything she did, from table setting, to her wardrobe, to home decor. A silly fight as we planned my wedding was over her desire to serve both a fruit salad and a lettuce salad to add another course to the meal. I thought she was putting on airs. She would have loved to see how formal and elaborate wedding planning became in the future.

I used to think it was because she grew up with little and wanted to rise above that. I suspect it may have deeper roots. When her father's family disowned him, did she internalize this message and believe she wasn't good enough, either? Was she  trying to rise above her father's legacy? I believe she had a complex sense of her own worth.

When I discovered there was a town called Ruthven in Ontario, I asked her if there was a connection. Her response was vague and uninterested, "maybe, I don't know" or "I don't think so." There was no "google" or "ancestry.ca" in those days to aid research, but that changed, and my exploration continued to reveal lots more about Mom's ancestors.

(1) (https://confessionsofanover-workedMom.com/the-legend-of-the-bayberry-candle/).

Chapter 24

Community of Ruthven

March 23, 1944
My Dear Wife: ... Bing Crosby has just come on the radio, and I love
you... Yours always, Murray.

Hugh and Emily (Fox) Ruthven

Mom told me once that her parents had thought about calling
her brother Adolph instead of Frederick. She was happy they
had not because of the legacy left by Adolph Hitler. She either
didn't know, or mention, that the name was a nod to her
grandfather, Adolphus Ruthven, who with her grandmother,
Elizabeth, left a positive impression in his community.

As did Adolphus' parents.

Adolphus was the only son of Hugh Ruthven and Emily Fox.
Here was a couple who earned their place in history when the
community of Ruthven was named after Hugh, the postmaster.
It was common at the time to name settlements after the
person who served in this position. Ruthven is about 26 miles
south and east of Windsor, close to the U.S. border.

Hugh and Emily's marriage brought together two pioneering
families that were instrumental in settling the area through

prolific childbearing, successful farming, and prosperous industries.

Hugh was 29 and Emily was 23 when they exchanged vows on May 21,1855. They had four children: Adolphus (Mom's grandfather) in 1856, Amelia in 1860, Cora in 1866, and Mary in 1870. Emily had a brother, Adolphus Skinner Fox, and he may have been the source of their only son's name. Tragedy struck this family as well when Cora died at 3, but a cause of death was not recorded.

A look at the ancestors who came before Hugh and Emily provided some insight into these early pioneering times. Stories my mother would have been proud to recount had she known.

Hugh's parents were Colin "Neil" Ruthven and Catherine MacColl who farmed in the County of Elgin. This couple married

in Craignish, Argyll, Scotland in 1809, and then immigrated. Neil's family remained in Scotland while Catherine came from a large family that also immigrated and settled in the Elgin area.

< *Catherine (MacColl) Ruthven's family stone in the Ford Cemetery on Talbot Line in West Elgin declares she was one of four brothers and five sisters who settled in the area.*

This great-great-grandmother of Mom's, Catherine MacColl, epitomized the strength of pioneering women. Married at age 19 in 1809, Catherine's first birthing experience produced a daughter in 1811. Twenty-five years later, in 1836, the 46-year-old mother gave birth to her last, and 8th child, another daughter. Hugh arrived 6th in line on Oct. 19, 1826, one of five boys and three girls. It appears all the children survived their mother's death at age 70, long enough for her to see the youngest child mature to 24 years of age.

As the son of these hard-working Scottish immigrants who established a solid foundation in a new country, Mom's great-grandfather Hugh displayed an industrious nature from a young age. He began teaching at 16 and worked as an educator. For a short time, he was also a bookkeeper. Then, he formed a partnership with John M. Wigle in a milling and shipping business in Ruthven. He established saw, grist, and carding mills in the area, accumulating a lot of property. As a result, he became widely known commercially and was successful in local

politics. Hugh eventually served as Reeve for Gosfield Township and was the first member of St. George Masonic Lodge at Kingsville. He died Oct. 31,1904, one month after his son's musical accomplishment at the World Fair in St. Louis.

< Hugh is buried in Kingsville, Greenhill Cemetery.

If property equals wealth, then Hugh may be the source of the family's good fortune, the "silver spoon" as my mother called it in her father's mouth; it may be why her grandparents, Adolphus and Elizabeth, could purchase the hotel in 1909.

Hugh was born in Canada, but our Canadian routes run deeper yet when we look at his wife. Mom's great-grandmother Emily Fox, like Hugh, came from a large farming family; she was the eldest of eight children born to Michael George Fox and Margaret (Peggy) Stewart. Like Catherine (MacColl) Ruthven, this great-great grandmother of Mom's spent 20 years having children, starting at age 21 with Emily in 1832, one year after being married, and ending in 1851. Sadly, their 8th child was stillborn when Margaret was 40. She lived until age 78 in 1889, survived by the rest of her children.

Emily's father died five years after her mother. The Reporter

in nearby Kingsville noted that Mom's great-great-grandfather Michael G. Fox "may be said to have been virtually the founder of Essex." (Funny how the accolades go to the men, but it was the women whose labour literally did the founding!)

< Michael George Fox

It is through this Fox line we add Germany to the ancestral mix of Scottish, Irish, and English roots. We go back to 1772 when Baden natives Philip and Catherine (Lamer) Fox left their home on the east bank of the Rhine River and sailed out of Liverpool to settle initially in Baltimore, Maryland. Then, with other German families, they slowly made their way north. By 1794, they drew lots on the lake shore in Gosfield South in the Essex County area of what would become Ontario.

Mom's great-great-great-great-grandparents Philip and Catherine Fox had their 10 children after immigrating. Their son George was born in the U.S., married Julianna Wigle after coming north with his parents, and lived on Pelee Island. The couple (great-great-great grandparents) had 12 children, all born in Canada; the oldest was Michael George (great-great-grandfather), who became father to Emily (great-grandmother).

Emily's mother, great-great-grandmother Margaret (Peggy) Stewart, was also born in the Essex area in 1811. A deeper look into her ancestry revealed a tale of uncommon courage and fortitude. Margaret was a daughter of Charles and Jennie Stewart (great-great-great-grandparents), and it is Charles' mother, also named Margaret, that we will look at next. This Margaret was Mom's great-great-great-great-grandmother. This was as deep as I ventured (keeping all the 'greats' straight gave me a headache!), but her story was too compelling not to add here, for future generations to be emboldened by the resiliency it shows. Many published records of the story allowed me to recreate it.

Chapter 25

A Tale of Pioneering Strength

Thursday, March 23, 1944
My Dear Wife: ... Do you realize you are impeding the war effort? The
instructor has to wake me up and bring me back to Mountain View
every once in a while. I'm always daydreaming, and you're always in
my dreams." Yours always, Murray.

Margaret (Brown) Stewart

Dunkard township, Greene County, Pennsylvania, circa 1790
Margaret secured the straps of her saddle bags and her rifle
again and walked a few steps to look the old gray steed in the
eyes. As she ran her gloved hand down the mane and tenderly
massaged the horse's ears, the horse shook her head and
snorted. As if in memory of the time young John pierced those
ears with the hot iron.

Margaret looked at the scars, remembering, and whispered to
the horse in sympathy, "He was a foolish lad, ah ken. Ah
remember poor James yelling he would skelp his wee behind."
She smiled, lost in thought for a few moments, then shook her
own head.

"But you'll serve me well on this trip, ken? We've many miles to

go, and I must find my boys." Margaret's voice rose in firmness, and as if in understanding, the horse gently nuzzled the mother's hand in response.

Margaret took a last glance at her remaining family on the porch of the house she and James had built: Charles and Daniel were standing tall, shouldering the responsibility she had forced on them. The three younger girls were crying as their older sister, Sophia, comforted them. "You ken your chores, take good care of each other, and keep a watch for each other. Keep the heid," she gave her orders in her brusque Scottish accent.

She worried about leaving them, but she thought back to the conversation she had three days ago. The traveller brought her news about a young lad, matching John's description, who had been seen over in Ohio. "You cannae no go there," he had told her. "I just told you so you would feel some peace, ken he's alive."

But she had thought of little else over the past few years than recovering her lost sons, ever since her husband's horrible death and the boys went missing, taken by the Shawnee. She laid her hand across her throat and bowed her head. Under her blouse, she felt the small parcel that hung around her neck, a lock of her husband's hair inside. She had gathered the bits of hair left behind after the scalping.

She mounted the horse, and with a gentle nudge, the mare faithfully began the long trip. It wouldn't be the first time Margaret Brown Stewart had travelled a distance by horseback, although this time she was alone. (She would become known as the first white woman to willingly cross the Alleghany Mountains when she came to the area with her husband.) It was not long after The Revolution when she and James came to settle their farm in Pennsylvania. She remembered the hardship of the trip that was combined with the excitement of establishing their family in this unfamiliar country of opportunity. They had left Scotland to find suitable land where they could farm and raise a family to have a future. That dream had been so close.

As the horse kept a steady trot, Margaret thought back to all that James had endured, pressed by force into service in Scotland when he was still very young. They placed him with the 42nd Highland Regiment, Black Watch, taking part in war against the French. Then, coming to America, he served as a colonel in the British army and took part in the Battle of Bunker Hill. They married and their family of four boys and four girls arrived. They established their farm with fields of wheat and a barn with pigs. But then a war of a different sort was upon them. In fear, they, along with many other families, took refuge in a fort about two miles from the farm, protected from native Indians who roamed the area and killed settlers, fighting against the white man invasion.

Her memories were disrupted by the sight of another traveller coming toward her. "Mrs. Stewart."

Her neighbour's young son was approaching. "Ma'am," he called again. "I have sommit for you from my ma." He reached into his bag and brought out a piece of paper and a red handkerchief tied around something bulky. "It's sommit to eat, and a letter for Ma's family, who are settled where you are going. Ma said this will introduce you, and that they will help you."

News seems to travel fast, even when people are sparsely settled, Margaret mused. But this was welcome support, and she thanked the lad as they parted. This was better than the time she had asked for help to thrash her wheat and her neighbour had refused, fearing that Indians would also kill her husband if he helped Margaret.

They had all lived in fear, staying in the fort, and tending to their farms as they could. The day James took their boys, young James and John, to tend to their livestock, they had understood the Shawnee were away, that it would be safe. They hadn't even taken their rifles. When they didn't return by the expected time, a rescue party assembled, but it was too late. Margaret found her husband's body, trampled by the livestock, and scalped. Small tufts of hair remained, and she gathered what she could. Her boys were gone.

Inconsolable in her grief, Margaret stayed at the fort for the next seven years with her young children. Eventually she found the strength to return to the farm, determined to bring the dream to life again for her family, and resolute about finding her lost sons. They would be young men now. She was relentless in asking anyone she met about her missing boys, which eventually led to this sliver of hope.

As mid-day approached, Margaret found a small creek and stopped for a break and to water her horse. She opened the wrapped parcel and smiled at the hunk of cheese, bread, and the slice of pie. After eating, she walked and stretched. Luckily, the day was warm and dry, the ruts in the path easy to follow.

Between roadside inns, and a couple nights of sleeping under the stars, Margaret reached her destination after several days.

She was exhausted, and the letter from her neighbour introduced her to a family in Batavia, where she was provided a comfortable place to sleep. She was up early the next morning to begin her search. Holding the horse's reins, she walked down the street and saw two young men carrying a crate of apples between them. The one at the far end looked familiar!

She approached him.

"John?" she said tentatively.

Then more confidently, "John Stewart." The lad looked like his *father, but there was no recognition in his eyes as he looked at her, and her heart began to break.*

"You dinna recognize me," she said. The lad, still looking puzzled, turned his attention from the woman to the horse she was leading, and a memory stirred. He walked over to the mare and reached his hand to its ear, where the piercing was evident. And a smile broke out on his face as he hugged the horse and then turned to look at Margaret again.

"You're my mother."

The story of Margaret Brown Stewart travelling on her own over such a distance to find her son is true and recorded in many forms. John recognized the piercing in the horse's ear before he knew his mother.

After finding John, Margaret learned more about what had happened to her sons in the intervening years. After witnessing their father's scalping by a band of Shawnee, John and James were taken and traded at Lake Erie to the Wyandottes who took them further north. They were adopted by the tribe only after they forced each to prove their worth through various tests, including running the gauntlet. James did well, but John was further tested when he was put into a cave with a bear and a rifle. He passed the test, but eventually John escaped and travelled south to Ohio to be found by his mother.

Margaret's search wasn't over when she found John; she still had to find James. After returning to the farm, John and Margaret planned a trip to look for him. Daughter Sophia and her husband agreed to look after the farm while Margaret and John travelled north to what is now the County of Essex in Canada where they believed James was still living with his captors. The trip involved travel through dense forest, around Lake Erie and then crossing the Detroit River by boat, swimming their horses. They arrived in what is now Amherstburg. They soon learned that James was no longer with the Indians. He was farming near Cedar Creek in Essex County, and a reunion followed.

After finding James, Margaret remained for about a year and then returned to the U.S. Her farm was again attacked by Indians who burned everything to the ground. In 1805, she

made the long trek back to Canada for a last time with all her family, as well as nine horses and one cow. She lived out the rest of her life in her daughter Sophia's home, dying at 107.

< Kingsville is where Margaret is buried and honoured on a stone that includes the Augustine family, also early settlers.

Sophia was widowed when she travelled north with her mother and married Abel Augustine after coming to Canada. A stone to honour these early settlers stands in the middle of a large corner lot surrounded by modern homes in Kingsville.

While the connection is distant, Margaret's story deserves to be shared and is proof of the strong stock in these pioneering families.

My mother knew nothing of her background, unfortunately. If she had seen who came before her father, and the deep roots her ancestors had in this part of the province, she may have been able to embrace genuine pride and risen to the challenges in her own life with more confidence.

Instead, she held onto a story about her maternal grandmother and the heartache of a poorly thought-out marriage that created Jessie Ruthven, her mother.

Chapter 26

A Debt Paid

March 23, 1944
My Dear Wife… Here comes Joey, the kid from New Toronto…. He just borrowed my nail file, and I still love you… Yours always, Murray.

Jessie (McDonald) Chalmers

"Don't name any of your children Jessie."

Mom gave this direction to her first grandson when he married in 1997, and that summed up her feelings for her mother. However, her grandmother was also named Jessie, and Mom recalled her fondly. In fact, there was one tale she shared about her maternal grandmother, Jessie McDonald.

According to my mother's story, Jessie McDonald had just immigrated to Canada from Scotland and came to an inn near Walkerton. She was on her own. An older woman, Elizabeth (Ruler) Chalmers, saw the predatory gaze the men at the inn were giving Jessie, and she became concerned. She invited the young woman to stay with her, and through the night, Jessie's room was indeed breached. Jessie was so grateful to her benefactor that a few years later, when Elizabeth Chalmers died leaving her husband William with five children, Jessie married him so she could care for Elizabeth's children.

It was challenging to locate any details that would corroborate this story. I learned that a daughter of William and Elizabeth Chalmers was born in Kincardine, and I wondered if, rather than Walkerton, it was the Walker House in Kincardine where the two women met. The Walker House operated as an inn and tavern in those days.

William Chalmers, who had emigrated in 1866 from Aberdeen, Scotland, worked for the railway as a locomotive engineer. It's plausible that he and his first wife, Elizabeth Ruler, who had their daughter Grace in Kincardine in 1882, had cause to be at the inn. The census lists them as residing in Kincardine in 1881 and his occupation as engine driver. Perhaps Elizabeth became concerned about Jessie, a single woman, and invited her into her home.

I believe my great-grandmother Jessie McDonald was a daughter of Duncan McDonald and Maggie McCrae born about 1852 and who left Glasgow, Scotland, in 1874 at 22. A passenger named Jessie McDonald is listed as a domestic on the vessel Canadian that docked in Quebec. It wasn't unusual at the time for single women to travel under that occupation. Domestic service is what many of them sought once here. The only proof I have of her whereabouts is her Bible that includes her signature and the date: "Toronto, Sept. 9, 1877." How Jessie came to leave Toronto is unknown; perhaps she was looking for work outside of the city or perhaps she decided to be adventurous and travelled by train to see the lake area outside of Toronto.

Regardless of how or where the two women met, Jessie McDonald married "Mr. Chalmers" as my mother referred to him, Nov. 20, 1889, and they had one child, my grandmother, whom they named Jessie Mary in 1891. But the union was not well thought out. According to my mother, the other children in the family were not accepting of their new sister, and "Mr. Chalmers was not a nice man." Jessie McDonald eventually left him and lived with Fred and Jessie; she is listed as a member of her daughter's household in the 1921 census. William Chalmers died a widower at 85 in 1933. His death certificate lists only one wife, Elizabeth Ruler. I could not uncover any records for my great-grandmother's death.

In summary, Fred Ruthven's family didn't approve of his marriage to Jessie Mary Chalmers. Aunt Peg thought her father's parents had someone else in mind for Fred before he married Jessie.

I am left to conjecture that since the Chalmers didn't have the long-established roots or community standing of the Ruthvens, and Jessie's family was known to be troubled, the marriage was opposed.

My mother was born into this dynamic of family disapproval, infant death, and excessive drinking on August 23, 1919. The family continued to experience frequent moves, a father out of work, an ill mother, and abuse.

For Mom, it seems life didn't really begin until 1935, when she spotted my father at their mutual place of employment-Campbell's. Were they soul mates? Was it love at first sight? Fate? Whatever the name, she knew it as soon as she saw him.

Ginger's life began to take shape away from her family's troubles as she transitioned from newlywed to motherhood to corporate wife, hand-in-hand with Murray as he climbed the chain of command and social hierarchy at work. Future dreams were coming true for the two kids who hailed from a poor, depression-era childhood.

We pick up the story of Murray and Ginger at the end of a brief six-month stay in their second home, purchased to accommodate the expanding family that had just welcomed its fourth son. There was barely time to unpack when Murray was transferred to the head office of Campbell's in Camden, New Jersey. The family prepared to move, without Sharon, south of the border. It was a significant chapter in my parents' lives.

Cousin Sharon O'Donovan, daughter of Aunt Bette and Johnny O'Donovan. With her mom (centre) and with my brother Rick on horseback.

Cousins Linda and Larry Ruthven, children of Mom's brother Larry and wife Giselle. I have no images of Tony, Bus' son. Dad's brother Jack (Uncle Nink), with his wife Phyllis, and their son Jimmy. Sharon standing beside Rick and Miles in the highchair around the time Sharon lived with us.

In later years, Dad (right) with brother-in-law Larry and partner Sally on a visit he and Mom took to LA post-retirement. Jan with Aunt Peg at his 1978 graduation from University of Guelph.

Chapter 27

Haddonfield

January 31, 1956
Darling Murray: Hello Honey, well what do you think of your ole
lady now, giving you a daughter to spoil. And I'll bet she will be spoilt.
We will have to watch ourselves. And as much as the boys complain,
I'll bet they will spoil little Kim too, won't they? … You can be sure
though that I am missing you like anything, and the kids. I'm dying to
find out what Jan said when he heard the news. I don't know just when
the Dr. is going to let me out, or when I can travel, but if I can make it
by next weekend, I'll be home darling, so have your arms waiting,
because that is what I want more than anything right now, is your
arms around me.

Kim

This is the only love letter I have written by my mother. Dad
saved it and gave it to me after I gave birth to my first child. I
treasure it, as I know he did. I find comfort in the lines that show
her excitement for having birthed a girl on January 29, 1956,
after four boys. Murray no doubt treasured the clear message of
Ginger wanting his arms around her.

The stories around my birth fascinated me, as they do most
children, but the fact we lived in Haddonfield added a unique

twist to my story. Mom wanted her own doctor, who had delivered all the boys, to attend this 5th birth. Thus, as the birth date approached, she flew home to Toronto with Miles, leaving Jan, Bill, and Rick at home with Dad. Dad was envious of her chance to fly. He used to take us to the Toronto airport when we were kids just to watch the planes take off. His math skills forced him into a navigator's role during the war, not the pilot's seat as he desired. It would have thrilled him to fly in the plane his son, Jan, built and piloted in later years.

"It's a girl, Ginger. It's a girl." So exclaimed Dr. Elliott, who was likely as surprised as my parents to discover my gender after four boys. Gender reveals before the birth were not a thing yet.

< Dad, Kim, and Miles

"I think he was more excited than I was," my mother deadpanned.

Dad said he was at the bowling alley and after he got the news, he claimed to roll a strike.

But the funniest memory told over the years was the homecoming. Mom, Miles, and I returned by train, and Dad had arranged for the three older boys to accompany him to the station. He was furious when he realized that Rick had wandered away to the far end of the platform, distancing himself from his family.

"It embarrassed him that his parents still had babies," my father laughed. Still having babies was Dad's euphemism for "having sex."

The move to the U.S. opened a new chapter in my parents' lives that had an enduring impact on the family. Not only did their fifth child and only daughter arrive, but lifelong friendships were seeded. Although it was a few years off, our cross-border ties were strengthened when Rick returned to attend Rutgers University in New Jersey and, upon graduation, marry Linda Bitler, his American sweetheart.

"You will probably meet and fall in love with an American," Dad told Rick as he prepared to move back to the U.S. for school. "I thought he was crazy," Rick told me. Perhaps Dad was thinking about how he fell in love with an American himself.

For my father, two-years shy of his 40th birthday, this move to the head office of Campbell Soup in Camden was the pinnacle of his career. I suspect they were heady times, particularly for my mother. The fur coat and silverware purchased during this time were tangible evidence of their success. Neither was aware of the dark days ahead.

One of the Super 8 movies from this time is of a house party and my mother, wearing a navy blue and white polka dot dress, dancing. She flashed a huge smile each time she and her partner swirled in front of the camera, likely held by my father. They took another Super 8 at Easter 1956 and it shows Mom holding me in a wobbly three-month-old sitting position on the coffee table. Miles repeatedly pops up to push the brim of my bonnet down, followed by Mom pushing it back up. Five pregnancies took their toll and Mom had been unwell for some time after returning home with me. Dad said he took this movie to celebrate both of us being up and about.

Chapter 28

The Taylors

April 19, 1944
My Darling… Hasn't the weather been good these last two days? It makes me think back to the time we had together on such bright days. Our 48 is in the bag Hon; so, I will be seeing you Thursday night.

Charlie and Fran Taylor

To make the move in 1953 to the U.S., Mom and the boys boarded a train in Toronto to join Dad, who was already working in New Jersey. Both Bill and Jan recalled the train ride that included a berth for sleeping; Jan thinks one of his first memories is of this trip because of the man who closed their curtains-it was the first Black face he had ever seen.

The move to the U.S. brought exposure to many differences, including races we had not interacted with previously in Canada. As the quieter reflective son, Jan was the one to take note. Three years later, as the family prepared to return to Toronto, it was five-year-old Jan who uttered the observation: "Annie's grandpa says they are buggers, but I don't think so, do you Dad? They are just people," as he watched the Black men from the moving company pack our belongings.

Jan was always a deep thinker, Dad said, and you never knew what might come out of his mouth. Dad could not see the movers, but he was acutely aware of the Black men through Jan's eyes.

"Out of the mouths of babes," he said in later years when he shared this memory. (1)

When Mom arrived in Haddonfield, she had her hands full with four boys, ages 12, 6, 2 and 1. On the day the movers showed up with the household effects, she was confronted with U.S. hospitality at its finest in the body of Fran Taylor. Fran was a 5-foot nothing ball of energy with a loud and distinctive north Jersey accent. She came to help and moved into our hearts. Her voice was slightly nasal with soft a's, although her 'water', which sounded like 'wodder' was more southern Jersey. The state has many variations in its accent, but the sound of it always makes me smile and feel at home - which is exactly what the Taylors did for the Dadsons.

"I'll take your boys for the day - I'm just next door (her r rolling to a soft doah). You focus on unpacking and getting settled," she directed, taking Miles into her arms, and leading the others back to her home. Childcare, dinner, all taken care of for the day. And so started a lifelong friendship; my girly wardrobe was enhanced thanks to Fran's sewing skills, and I was a flower girl at their daughter's wedding in 1962. We considered Auntie Fran and Uncle Charlie as family, and they were invited to all our weddings. Their home had a screened-in porch across the front and in my memory, they filled their house with big comfortable chairs, human kindness, love, lots of people, and laughter. And it's always hot. I had to dress in front of a fan for my flower girl duties.

We were not the only visitors the Taylors welcomed into their home. When their children attended university, they usually brought home foreign students who had no home on

holidays. Auntie Fran became a second mom to a family of Chinese students and in later years she travelled to China to meet the family. "We could not speak each other's languages, but the family was gracious and wonderful to us," she said of the visit.

< Kim and Auntie Fran on one of their visits north

I recall the people who were special friends to our parents over the years-Sam and Marg Maxwell, Ross and Phyllis Gimblet, Charlie and Fran Taylor, and in later years in Listowel, Jack and Ev Reis. My parents had a capacity to welcome people into their circle, broadening the definition of family.

We often travelled back to visit the Taylors. A long trip, it usually involved a stay in a motel where the sound of the transport trucks on the highway lulled me to sleep. To pass the time in the car, we played I Spy, or sang Down by the Bay.

"Down by the bay where the watermelons grow
Where the watermelons grow
I dare not go, I dare not go
For if I do, For if I do
My mother will say My mother will say
Did you ever see (insert a silly rhyme such as "a turtle
wear a Playtex girdle" or "a snake eat a cake"
Down by the bay!"

We still recall with much laughter the tension in the car as we approached the Canadian border. Mom would have shopped for children's clothing, removed the tags, and packed them in the suitcases. My father, burdened with the need to be completely honest, would get anxious. He would be given strict orders by mom, "Just be quiet and don't say anything. I will do the talking." It seemed to work as I don't recall any issues for us as we crossed and as kids, we would cheer once we came upon the Canadian flag on the Peace Bridge.

I could always count on Dad for one story while we were on routes with walls of towering rock formations on either side of the road. Posted signs read: Watch for Falling Rock.

"Do you know who Falling Rock is?" Dad asked. "He was an Indian brave who was in love with the Indian Chief's daughter." My little woman's heart loved this story, and Dad continued despite groans from my brothers. "Falling Rock was not the only Indian Brave to be in love with the Chief's daughter. She was very beautiful, and many were interested, but eventually it came down to two: Falling Rock and Flying Eagle. So, one day the wise Chief called the two braves and told them they had to prove their worth if they wanted his daughter as their wife. The brave who returned with the most and best quality furs would win her hand in marriage. The two Indian braves set out on their hunt, and after several weeks passed, Flying Eagle returned to the camp. He was sure he would have more furs than Falling Rock. The Chief counted the furs and agreed it was an impressive hunt. But they had to wait for Falling Rock. And they waited. And they waited. And to this day, the wait continues. That is why you see signs 'Watch for Falling Rock'."

(1) For a further reflection on race, please read the Author's Notes.

Rick holds his little brother Bill. Bill and Jan dress-up like daddy–including pipes. A birthday celebration. Rick is at end of the table with Jan in front of him. Bill stands beside Miles who is in the highchair. Neighbourhood guests at the party in the middle. Mom always made birthdays special. You could choose what kind of cake and ice cream you wanted. The full gang in 1959 in Toronto with 1 unknown neighbour kid. Rear in the middle, Rick with Bill to his right. Front from left: Miles, Jan, and Kim.

Chapter 29

Back to Canada

Thursday, March 23, 1944
"My Dear Wife: ... I love you for many things, among them the many fond memories. I think of the silly little things we used to do together, and they seem so important to me now. I love you Hon.

Kim

The move back to Toronto was to a story-and-a-half home on Harvest Drive in Toronto. Rick was in high school and recovered from the embarrassment experienced by a sister's birth. He had discovered that a baby sister could be great chick bait. He and his friend, John Wheatley, took me out with them. While it helped Mom, what they didn't tell her was that I was often dropped off with John's mother, who enjoyed looking after a little girl. I don't remember this at all, but learned about it years later when, in one of those odd twists of fate, I ended up working for John some 30 years later.

My own memories of this time are fleeting as I grew from baby to toddler to little girl ready for school. In one memory, I can see the backs of two men wearing white shirts, and I feel responsible for the frustration I sense radiating off them. I believe it was Dad and Rick putting a play stove together for me on a Christmas morning.

What I remember of my mother is warm and loving. I recall getting dressed up and attending an outdoor tea with her in someone's backyard, where there were several tables with umbrellas set and a delicious lunch served. Cucumber sandwiches come to mind with this memory.

I also have a vivid image in my mind of being in a clothes closet, jackets and coats hanging around my head. I look down at my feet and I see locks of blonde hair falling to the floor. That's my memory, but the fact I had cut my hair was captured in a photograph of me in a pretty dress and boasting a pixie haircut. I can still feel how the crinoline of those dresses would tickle my legs.

I also remember standing at the front door of this home, looking outside. It is pouring rain, but I can see a sign on our lawn, and somehow, I know it means we are moving to another house. I am excited by the thought.

But, as I reflect, that dismal rain heralded changes that would have some lasting negative impacts on our family. None of us knew of the changes to take place over the next few years, but around this time, Rick had already returned to the U.S. to attend Rutgers as the rest of the family prepared to move to Chatham. Oddly enough, back to an area of the province closer to my mother's ancestral roots. The upcoming moves from Toronto to Chatham to Listowel were part of a chain of events and details that are still shrouded in some mystery, because this time, neither my mother nor my father talked about them.

Chapter 30

The Plant

Thursday, March 23, 1944
"My Dear Wife: ... Did you make a mistake when you married me Hon? Are you sorry? I know I have left you with a lot of worry and responsibility and it bothers me. I will owe you so much by the time I get back, that it will take all my life to repay... Yours always, Murray."

Murray and Ginger

The sense of debt my father felt after two years of service with the RCAF extended beyond his devotion to my mother, as expressed above. Campbell Soup saved his job while he was away, and he became solidly loyal to his employer. But his 45 years there had consequences for our family, some that might be anticipated while others were a tense undercurrent that was felt in different ways by each of us.

You could say our family was rooted in Campbell's. Not only did my parents meet at the Toronto plant, but this was also where my brother Jan eventually worked for 13 summers. Mom's sister Peg enjoyed a full career of over 25 years in the Toronto office before her own retirement. Their father worked

as a guard for a while. My brother Miles worked for a short period at the Listowel plant. When Dad died, each of us received one of his Campbell's pins that marked his years of service. As the youngest I have his 20-year pin.

< THE Campbell Soup Kids on a Christmas tree ornament!

We were Campbell Soup kids. Christmas parties for children were huge affairs, and I vividly recall the awe of approaching the big man in the red suit and white beard. We ate only Campbell's tomato soup and tasted many of their new frozen products in our home. In later years, my parents regularly attended the annual 25-year party, always a night over in a downtown Toronto hotel with a meal and dance, time to visit old friends and colleagues.

< Ginger at a 25-year party in her late 40s – early 50s.

One year, they came back with a funny story. Dad had gone to the bar to get a tray of drinks for their table. While waiting for the drinks, a woman approached him.

"Oh Murray, I remember you and your bedroom eyes."

Dad joked about chatting with this woman he said he did not recognize, but he enjoyed the attention. When he got back to the table, he discovered he was minus one drink, which he assumed, with a lot of self-deprecating chuckling, she took. This was a bit of a twist on the usual stories that followed events they attended. Dad always boasted about how attractive Mom was and what a hit she was on the dance floor. She took pride in the fact people thought she looked younger than her age.

The Toronto plant was Campbell Soup's first Canadian operation, opened in August 1931 in Long Branch, where my parents' families lived just off Lakeshore Drive. Dad would be about 16 when it opened, still in high school. His parents supported their children in completing high school, so it was four years later in 1935 when he began at Campbell's.

"He started at Campbell's because of the size of his arm," Jan noted. Dad was among people who stood in front of the plant each day hoping to get picked for work. While he may have looked strong enough to get his foot in the door, once there, he worked hard to stay.

< Murray (right) taste-testing at Campbell's

Dad was always proud that he completed high school at Mimico High and would have loved to go further, but there was no money for this dream. It was important to him that his children all had the chance he was denied. Instead of university, he found Campbell's, where they supported his vision for a better future with professional development courses, including ones on food preparation at MIT. They also provided training in the then-current analytics about how to choose the right people for career pathways. Dad was also a founding member of the Toronto Toastmaster's club, signalling his desire to improve skills in support of his career.

His efforts paid off and my father became superintendent of Canadian operations; they transferred him to the head office in Camden, New Jersey, and then returned him to Toronto three years later, about six months after I was born in 1956.

The next transfer to Manager of the Chatham plant occurred in four years, 1960. The last move was to Listowel in 1963 where the plant produced Swanson frozen dinners and Pepperidge Farm products. We often got to taste-test frozen dinners at home. Years later, someone made a disparaging remark about a woman for serving frozen dinners to her family, and it startled me. I never associated eating prepared meals with my mother's housekeeping skills. We were taste-testers of new products!

The first I learned that Dad's relationship with Campbell's was not all rosy, I was in elementary school in Listowel. I asked Bill, "Why doesn't Mom want to do anything?"

"What do you mean?"

"I have to beg her to attend meet-the-teacher nights at school. When I asked her to come to the school play, she told me, 'I would if you had a bigger part.'"

The fact she attended a Grade 8 music concert where I was to sing a duet with Linda MacDonald was so special, I ended up with laryngitis from nerves, five minutes before the performance. Classic case of stage fright, prompted in part because of the attention from Mom.

Bill explained: "Something terrible happened to Dad at work, and that's why we moved to Listowel. It's why Dad works nights. Dad's salary was cut, and they can no longer afford some things they did before. Like Mom going to the hair salon. People that they thought were friends won't have anything to do with them.

They stopped talking to them.

"Mom is depressed," he said.

Dad's work was not a topic of discussion at home. In fact, I never knew he was head of Canadian operations until I read correspondence while writing this memoir. Bill was the oldest at home when this story unfolded, and in later years, he provided this detail.

"Rick was in Camden at Rutgers University and the rest of you were too young. The story I was given by Mom is that someone in the plant sent an order to water down the product. Dad objected to the proposed changes, or there was a set-up of some sort, and he was moved around with the intent of making him quit.

"When Dad accepted the transfer to Listowel, it was with a 1/3 cut in salary and demotion to afternoon shift. They didn't even cover his moving costs."

Jan says that every summer he worked at Campbell's in Toronto, someone would come up to him and ask if he was Murray's son; they would then ask Jan to say hello, to tell Dad they admired him, and to pass along the message: "Damn the bastards." According to Jan's sources, it was someone who had been a family friend who deliberately watered down the V8 juice, and when it had to be thrown out, they pointed the finger at Dad.

Trying to read between the lines of history again, I wondered whether some considered Dad a part of the 'old guard' that started with the company in its early years. He had no formal education behind him that perhaps others interested in climbing the ladder acquired. For sure, Dad would not have tolerated playing office politics and could be honest to a fault. I know there was stress. With adult eyes, I now look back on an incident in Chatham when Dad threw my play kitchen table across the back lawn in anger. It had toppled over and spilled a meal Mom had placed on it. Bill speculated that the trouble began even before Chatham and that the move from Toronto was only the start.

While the specifics of who, what, and why are obscured with time, Dad worked the afternoon shift in Listowel for 10 years-from the time I was in Grade 3 to my final year of high school. Then he finished his career as Assistant Manager of Maintenance and Engineering when he retired in 1980. Dad had little choice but to keep working and supporting his family. His eldest son was in university, and with four more kids he wanted educated, he had little alternative than to keep his chin up and keep working at Campbell's. Mom told me he tried to look for other work, but at his age-late 40s and early 50s-it was impossible. They were of the generation that believed in loyalty to employers and would not have considered changing jobs so easily, despite the poor treatment. She described Dad as a company man.

What I do remember is that Dad always claimed Listowel was the best thing that ever happened to him. He loved the small town, the big old house they purchased there, and the people. Lemonade from lemons. So, in the end, he won. But all five of us kids have, at one time or another, or as a life's career choice, gone into our own businesses. It was subliminal, as my parents did not teach it as a family value, but a major message we absorbed was that when you work for someone else, you don't control your life.

The depression Mom experienced, and the fact she never really reconciled to living in Listowel, show how deeply affected she was by what happened. Mental health was not the topic it is today when people are better at recognizing the signs and symptoms. Mom just silently suffered.

I believe her depression reflected how closely her self-esteem was connected to Dad. For that time and generation, it was not unusual for a wife to be tied to her husband's career, yet I now believe, as I reflect on Mom's life and family, that the only esteem she had was derived from her position as Mrs. Murray Dadson. She rode with him to the heights of his career, and she was with him when it seemingly crashed. Dad's family background, raised by parents who loved him unconditionally, provided him with a healthy self-esteem that enabled him to not only survive the fall, but to rise above it. He became a beloved supervisor at the Listowel plant, and when he retired, they named one of the meeting rooms after him. Mom, on the other hand, didn't have that strong foundation. She was scarred badly when the Dadson's were dropped from the "A" list of Campbell elite. I wonder if for Mom, was it also an echo of Ruthven family disdain, of being told again that you don't measure up? It was a real challenge for her to move on, and her unhappiness permeated a good piece of my life.

I had never put the word 'courage' and Dad's life together, but the move to Listowel (whatever the cause) was clearly designed to pull the carpet out from underneath him. He landed on his feet with his head held high. His resiliency in the face of such a setback is a lesson in courage.

Chapter 31

Names

April 18, 1944
My Darling: … I am in the classroom now. It is now ten a.m., and I
have just got out of bed. The class is starting now, Hon, so I will sign
off for an hour or so. I love you, Murray.

Miles and Kim

Listowel, circa 1972

"You're Miles' sister."

I imagine it's the bane of many younger siblings that they
become known as the "sister or brother of" rather than by their
own names. In school, teachers can develop expectations
because of an older sibling. I remember the sinking feeling when
my English teacher Mrs. Pratt confirmed if I was Jan's sister.

'Miles' sister' was the most common moniker I got in
Listowel. Jan didn't tell anyone he had a younger sister, and I
was under strict orders to not acknowledge or speak to him
when I arrived at high school. Bill was just that much older I
didn't hamper his reputation, and he only spent a year in
Listowel before he left for university, seldom to return to town
again. Rick was already living in the U.S. and then he married in

1965; few people in Listowel even knew about an older sibling. When he returned to visit, he tried to parent me instead.

But the association with my brother Miles wasn't necessarily negative. When we moved to Listowel, I remember my mother telling him to go out and find some friends for me. I was shy, he was Mr. Personality. When I tried to tell a joke, my parents shook their heads. Miles got the laughs. But having a brother co-ordinate your social networking could have its advantages. He introduced me to the man who became my husband.

But before that, he may have protected me without knowing it. When I was a teenager, I had, foolishly, left the local bar with a couple of guys I just met. On our way to the party, somewhere in the country, I was chatting away when one said, "You're Miles Dadson's sister?" Not sure what I said to prompt this revelation, but I could tell it changed a dynamic in the truck cab. After a short time at the party, they safely delivered me home.

My name from birth was Roberta Kim; not expecting a girl, the planned name was Kim, regardless of my gender. I don't know if Robert was the male version, but my mother claimed that Roberta came from a little girl called Bobbie. That was her plan, but it never took, and I was Kim, or Kimmy, from the start. All of us had the "y" added to our names: Ricky, Billy, Jany, Milesy and Kimmy.

Except Dad sometimes called me Roberta Kim. Not when I was in trouble, and not all the time, but occasionally, rather as a way of showing love and affection for the "me" he had named.

I think of Roberta Kim as my true name. Dadson was my father's name and Denstedt is my husband's. Roberta Kim is mine.

Chapter 32

Not the Parents

Thursday, Aug. 10, 1944
Darling Ginger, … I love you, miss you, and want you with every
breath I take… Love, Murray

Murray and Ginger

Sex life and parents should be a non sequitur, I suppose. And compared to the messages that young lover's text and email each other in this century, my father's letters do appear tame. Writing that he 'wants' her is about the closest his writing comes to suggesting a sex life between them.

Jokes about sex, particularly what might be deemed risqué or vulgar, were not told in our house. I always felt it was about respecting the topic. One story Mom told contained hints of sex. She and my father met in Montreal during the war when he had a weekend furlough. Her sister, Peggy, unexpectedly showed up at their hotel door as her own plans to "meet a man," in my mother's words, had fallen through. Mom was so angry she made her sister sleep in the bathtub. But I didn't miss the disdain in my mother's voice when she recounted what her sister was doing there: meeting someone outside the bounds of marriage.

Dad sometimes teased that every time he hung his pants on the bedpost, Mom got pregnant again. Mom just tsked. It was also a bit of family lore that 15-year-old Rick was embarrassed when Mom brought me home from the hospital. He said it was because he knew there would be no vacation again that year.

< All of us for Jan and Kathy's wedding, 1975. Rick and Jan standing. From left: Bill, Kim, Dad, Mom, and Miles.

I asked many questions about the topic, and considering her background, I credit Mom for her attempts to address me in a straight-forward manner. The fact I went to Mom to get the facts speaks volumes.

She told me that before she got married, she "sort of knew" what was coming but when she asked her mom, and then her married sister for information, she was brushed off. She wanted to provide a better response for me.

Although the first time I asked, "Mom, where do babies come from?" she tried to deflect the question with a response about flowers and seeds.

But the kids I played with had told me that "something goes through the air from the man's belly to the woman's." I shared a room with my brother, albeit there was a sliding door between us, and I was concerned. I needed to know.

"Really Mom. Where do babies come from?" I pressed. So, she told me, even using proper terminology, with this response from me:

"What's a penis?"

Some 50-plus years later, my granddaughters at age 4 could tell me, "That's my 'gina." And they knew what their brother's penis was called too.

Mom assured me that sex was a beautiful expression of love between a husband and wife and not to think it was terrible.

I told my children it was an expression of love between a man and a woman; my 8-year-old granddaughter told me that sometimes men can love men and women can love women. And that her parents lived together before they were married, like her aunt and uncle.

I recall Mom's raised eyebrows when I enthusiastically responded to her description of sex. "It sounds wonderful." As I matured, the tenor of the conversations changed.

"You will be disappointed.

"Men are not responsible for their behaviour. If they see a naked woman, they can't help themselves."

I argued with her about this. We should hold men responsible.

I have wondered since: was this message internalized as a way of excusing her father?

When I was at university and my then-boyfriend Jim came to visit for a weekend, she phoned.

"Where will he sleep?"

I told her I wasn't about to put him in the common room when there were four other women who shared the unit with me.

"You're a bitch on wheels," she said. No conversation about whether I took any precautions against pregnancy.

Oddly, when my father heard Jim would be making the trek to

Toronto rather than me coming home, he commented, that's good. We were never sure sometimes if Dad was like an absent-minded professor unaware of what was going on around him, or if he simply trusted us more. I took it as trust and never wanted to disappoint him.

Dad often said that he and Mom "came up the hard way," both of them innocent and having to learn along the way. When I tried to suggest they must have had sex before marriage, pointing out the trip up north they took with married friends, Marg and Sam Maxwell, she was adamant. Marg and Sam were chaperones and no, there was no sex. Some people might scoff, but I believed her and still do.

Their backgrounds did little to prepare them for a son's revelation some 40 years later, yet their response tells much about them.

Chapter 33

Bill

Listowel, Oct. 6, 1989
Dear Bill:
Just a little something for you to get a supply of food in your freezer.
Seeing as the others get a little something for their anniversary, we
thought to send you some too. Hope it will help a little. We do hope and
pray that things will turn out right for you. Please keep us informed,
even if we do worry about you, we would like to know. Love, Mom.

Bill

Kitchener, 2015

The first thing I noticed was the proper table setting for one. A ceramic dinner plate sat between a knife on the right and a fork on the left. Just above the fork was a bread-and-butter plate. It reminded me of my mother's precise instructions when we set the dining room table at home.

But this proper place-setting looked incongruous in a kitchen where grease and coffee stains spattered the cupboards. Some doors were off-kilter or mismatched with loose knobs. The table sat on an oval braided carpet, which might have looked homey, except for the worn and faded linoleum under it. On one side of the kitchen, an exposed set of stairs led to attic rooms. The landlord filled every nook and cranny in this rooming house with revenue. Bill's tiny room, tucked in the front corner, was next to a scummy bathroom I avoided.

I thought about Dad's nightmare of ending up in a 6 by 9-foot room. Bill was living in it.

I was glad my parents could not see where Bill was living, even if the proper table setting was stark evidence of who raised him. I wasn't sure if I wanted to laugh or cry at the sight of it.

Bill had started dinner preparations while I shopped for him. I trudged up to the second floor where he was living with plastic bags of groceries grasped in both hands, trying to avoid the grime on the walls on either side of the enclosed stairwell. I was helping him move the bags to the front of the kitchen cupboards, where he could more easily access them.

"Wow, that was fast. Thank you, Kim. You can do this much faster without me," Bill said as he emptied the bags, holding onto the counter to maintain his balance. He never forgot to express his thanks.

"No problem," I replied as my eyes travelled around the Kitchener rooming house. We had moved him here when he lost his apartment in Toronto. This was all he could afford. I worried. If there was a fire, he would never make it out. The thought kept me awake at night.

Since arriving at the seedy rooming house, Bill's condition had progressed to the point that he needed a walker. A bicycle lock protected the walker against theft on the front porch at the bottom of the steps. Upstairs, he relied on the walls and furniture to balance himself. To get downstairs, he held the railing with both hands and took one slow step at a time. It's why he suggested I shop without him from now on. This is the brother I used to have to run to keep up with as he strode along the sidewalk with his long legs.

<Rick, Bill, Kim, Miles, Jan. Rare when all 5 of us gathered in one place.

My life has been defined by the fact I had four older brothers. This was Bill.

When I was in Grade 2, I was at home sick with a severe cold. Bill was the brother who came in to see me at the end of his school day. Such attention from an older brother was memorable enough, but the one occasion I recall involved him turning up the volume on the radio beside the bed and telling me to listen to the music because the band was great. "Love, love me do, You know I love you." Bill's music tastes became my music tastes: The Beatles; The Everly Brothers; Peter, Paul, and Mary; Nana Mouskouri; and Simon and Garfunkel to name a few.

Bill was the brother whose bedroom in our Chatham home was on the lower level next to the family room. He teased me he would get to see Santa Claus on Christmas Eve and no, I could not sleep there with him.

Bill was the brother who took me trick or treating, patient while I knocked on the doors on one side of our street. But he would not wait for me to collect more candy from the houses on the other side on our way back home. I had enough candy, he said, and while likely true, I suspect he was in a rush to get to his own party with high school friends.

He hosted parties at the house, complaining to Mom when I sat at the top of the stairs to watch the older people in the rec room. I remember a similar house party in Listowel, where he tried to make friends despite the move so late in his school years. He told me he was part of a close-knit group of friends in Chatham, and those ties were broken when Dad transferred to Listowel.

Mom told me that they should have left Bill to finish high school in Chatham, as the move was tough on him. A psychologist they consulted after moving to the U.S. told them Bill did not tolerate change explaining why his school grades were negatively impacted each time they moved. We saw this adverse reaction to change a few times. He didn't leave Toronto until they forced him out of the apartment for unpaid rent and convincing him to accept a move from the second floor to the more accessible first floor in the rooming house felt like high stakes negotiation.

Chatham is where 17-year-old Bill earned his Queen Scout designation-the highest honour a scout can earn. He received it in 1964 from his Honour R.E. Rowe, Lt. Governor of Ontario, in a ceremony the family attended at Sarnia Central Collegiate. This honour, Bill told me, was his proudest accomplishment.

Bill was the brother who set me up on a blind date, even supplying the fake ID and encouraging me. "You look old enough, just don't talk or they will know you are younger." Quietest date ever.

And he is the brother who emailed me a recording of Paul McCartney singing "When I'm 64" on my 64th birthday because he knew I would appreciate it.

Bill studied art history at McMaster University but took a year off to travel through Europe, with my parents' support. When he returned, he set up a photography business, and his wedding gift to me and two of his brothers was the wedding photography. But around this time, he distanced himself from family; when I complained about him not coming home for Christmas, Mom told me she had excused him because he told her he got depressed at Christmas.

I remember when I heard the truth about Bill. Mom and I were dining at a restaurant on our way home from a business trip I made; Mom had joined me to keep me company on the road. We talked about Bill, and I stated that just because he was not married did not mean he was gay.

"He is, Kim," she told me.

Oh.

"He told your dad and I a while ago."

Wow. She knew. And I didn't.

Furthermore, she and Dad had known for a while, and it had not become a family crisis. A few years later, she told me that while she knew Bill was gay, she didn't believe he had sex with other men. Some form of denial, perhaps. Bill told me he had shared with her once how hurt he was after a relationship ended, and her quiet response had been, "Oh, it's the same."

Bill invited Mom and Dad to dinner in his apartment the night he planned to tell them. "Mom cried," he said. He gave her a book that told her it was not her fault.

"Dad got angry at first."

But they insisted on staying the night with him, the news too important to just leave. Bill and Dad left in the elevator to get a parking permit for the car.

"I'll tell you one thing. I think you've got a lot of guts," Dad said to him.

Bill considered that the highest compliment Dad ever gave him. Dad also told him, "I still love you." After that, when Bill came home, my father seemed to go out of his way to hug Bill. He clearly wanted to send the message that he did still love him. There may have been some sorrow as well, that this could make life more difficult for this son.

Bill was the brother with whom I could have deep and wide-ranging conversations, some lasting late into the night. Some of those conversations were about sexuality, a topic he evidently gave a lot of thought. He talked about the prevalence of homosexual behaviour throughout history. He detailed his belief that our feelings for other people of the same sex are on a continuum, and we all experience a level of same-sex affection; it's why we can be friends with each other. In those who identify as gay or lesbian, the feelings go beyond friendship and are sexual.

Perhaps, as I was his sister, he felt more comfortable sharing some of his life with me; he never told his coming-out story to our brothers. When I visited, he took me to Woody's, a large gay bar in Toronto, and to a smaller neighbourhood-type bar where there was a singing competition for drag queens. He proudly introduced me as his sister to friends, and I remember feeling some comfort in realizing he was safe as a part of this community. Like my parents, I worried about his safety. Bill was not a large man; he was tall but very slim, and there was a vulnerability about him.

Canada legalized same sex marriage in 2005, and he saw this

as something that would fundamentally impact the promiscuous behaviour that he noted was prevalent in the gay community.

"When you are viewed as deviant by society, then that excuses or provides permission for deviant behaviour. When who you are is acceptable to mainstream society, then there may be more of an inclination to live up to that with your behaviour."

I wonder if his choice of the word 'deviant' reflected how he may have viewed himself. How much it impacted other areas of his life is a guess. His life was not easy, and he made many poor business decisions; he was frequently in arrears on rent, and we knew Mom supported him, sometimes not always with Dad's knowledge. He sometimes did not eat or did not eat well as he didn't have the money. Cigarettes would be purchased before food or other necessities. When Miles and my husband helped Bill move out of his Hamilton apartment, they watched as Mom paid the city official who showed up prepared to take action if he did not pay a large bill for parking tickets.

Bill also gravitated toward people who had dysfunctional lives in different ways. I think in his effort to accept those who lived on the fringes of society, he forgot about his own boundaries, to his own detriment. He had a sympathetic heart and people took advantage of that. He told me he had not realized how fortunate we were to have the parents we did until he got out in the world and met other people and learned about their lives. He's not the only one to realize our lives were protected in some ways. I wonder perhaps if he was always balancing this deviant label with the mutual love and respect between himself and our parents who embodied traditional unions.

Bill had the upmost respect for our parents. For their 50th wedding anniversary celebration in 1990, one of Bill's friends told him he should take a date, but Bill refused.

"The party is about Mom and Dad, not me. I would if I had someone permanent in my life, but if I took a date, it would shift attention to me, away from them, and that's not what the party is about."

My parents accepted my brother, and if he had ever brought a partner home, I believe they would have found it in their hearts to accept that as well.

In an odd twist of fate, Bill's saving grace ended up being a heart-wrenching diagnosis he received while he still lived in Toronto. Cerebellar atrophy was a blow as it negatively impacted his effort to find work in graphic design, a skill he went back to school to learn later in life. The condition caused the slow loss of muscle coordination and balance; the diagnosis thankfully afforded him a disability pension that supported him for the last 15 years of his life. Genetics or the environment can cause the condition; when he explained it to me, he said the doctor told him it was from years of malnutrition.

While that was likely due to poverty, I speculate whether the intestinal issues I have discovered in our family lineage may have played a role. Around the family dinner table, I was the "good" eater while Mom was often prodding Bill to eat more, which he refused to do. We used to tease him that he needed a sweater to keep the wind from blowing him away on the street. He shared with me years later that it was embarrassing for him as a man to wear short sleeve t-shirts which exposed his thin arms.

Eventually, he needed a walker to get around, even the small bachelor apartment we found for him when his rooming house landlord decided to rent the space to a business and kicked him out. It was an improvement over the boarding house room he lost, but not easy. As noted, Bill did not like change.

He was, however, resilient and remained incredibly positive, despite the six steps that prevented him from leaving his home. He practiced his photoshop and design skills, played solitaire, and watched movies on his computer screen. He proudly managed on his own. He cooked for himself in his closet-sized kitchen. Bill was a voracious reader, ordering seven books at a time to be delivered by the library. We learned there isn't much that can't be delivered to the door. As his mobility decreased, he quickly learned how to hook up with what he needed to remain independent and reduce his dependence on me. He developed relationships with the people he connected with at a grocery store, a laundromat, the beer store, and, yes, black market cigarettes.

He was eating regularly for the first time in years. Jan, Miles, and I provided any additional support he required until the end at 74, when he died of pancreatic cancer. It was less than four months between diagnosis and death. I regret we argued in that time; he was determined to die in his own bed, alone. I sought home care which he refused, even though it would help keep him at home. He preferred his independence and lone-wolf status. He didn't quite get his wish after a nasty fall and a long, frightening night on his apartment floor. But he was at peace with the doctor's directions and cared for in the end in hospice.

My brothers and I mourned the lonely path that Bill walked in life, although we saw parts of his life reflected in the photo albums we found in his apartment. There were images of his team in the gay bowling league in Toronto's Village, trips south, and parties with friends. He's laughing in one, and I realized how seldom I saw this side of him in later years.

But we also saw the missed potential. My brother had an

incredible memory and was a brilliant conversationalist if the topic was about the history of the British royal family, art, old movies, or the latest historical book he was reading. I told him he should have been a history or English professor. We had many discussions about books and their metaphors, and the depth of discussions with him always left me feeling better informed about something!

The morning he died, a nurse at the palliative hospital told me she had been looking forward to talking to him again about old movies, Marilyn Monroe, and Andy Warhol, but he had quickly slipped into the next sphere.

We honoured his life and fervent direction to not bury him in Listowel. Instead, we remembered him with a tree in a Memorial Circle at Blue Springs Scout Reserve near Milton.

As his sister, I wish he had found that special someone who could have been a match to his intelligence and a life partner who would help him be the best version of himself. Someone who would have given him the self-respect and dignity he deserved under his wings. Like our parents.

Chapter 34

Through the Years

August 13, 1944
...Say Ginger one thing I wanted to ask you. Who made those socks
that were in the bundle I got? Are they the ones that Miss Galloway
made for me? P.S. I love you.

Murray and Ginger

Chatham feels like a brief hiatus in my memory. It's where I started school, learned to read and where mom put Miles and I into tap dance classes. Rick was a blur that I only vaguely remember. He doesn't come into focus for me until he gets married in 1965. Bill introduced me to the Beatles! I recall Jan catching a snapping turtle from the creek we used to cross on our way to school. The turtle clung to the end of a long stick, and he brought it to school for everyone to see. Miles and I were in the same room in the two-room school we attended, Jan in the senior room. Bill attended the high school that was across the field.

The creek at the end of our street played a role in a memorable incident in which a friend's sister fell through the ice. Thankfully, the creek wasn't that deep, as we just stood on the bank and yelled for her to get out. She did. We brought her home and my friend put her sister's clothes into the dryer in hopes of avoiding a confrontation. I don't know if or when the story came out, but I was impressed she knew how to operate the dryer. I'd never get away with that at home.

Older brothers participated in more dangerous play. Jan and his friends used to ride the ice flows on the creek and race each other. Further down from where we crossed the creek for school, the water ran under a double tunnel. The piece of ice he and a friend shared went sideways and became stuck under the tunnel. There was about a 2-foot clearance above their heads, so the water was deeper. They were able to break the ice into two pieces and each came out the other side successfully. But Jan was in his 40s before he told Mom about this escapade.

On the other hand, there were hijinks that didn't escape notice. Jan and friends were caught by the police putting stones and rocks on the train tracks. When Dad opened the front door, there was no "how dare you accuse my son" but rather "what did he do?" and likely some form of punishment followed. Jan doesn't remember what it entailed.

I remember being kept after school one day and having to sing Happy Birthday to one of the boys in the class because I, and a friend, didn't sing when the class did. He came from a poorer family and the teacher, in her wisdom, sought to teach us a lesson. I was mortified.

There was no corporal punishment in our house, but consequences followed if we misbehaved. While we all knew our parents supported us, we also knew they wouldn't brook poor behaviour.

Also, our parents were of the generation that didn't believe in unadulterated praise of their children. Years later when Jan spoke as the high school valedictorian, they did not stand and applaud with the rest of the crowd. That would show too much pride. They humbly expressed their joy at home.

I was in Grade 3 when another transfer was planned. This time it was Mom and I who travelled by train to this new location, and the family lived in a hotel just outside of town while we waited for the house to be ready.

Moving to the small, rural town of Listowel in 1963 was not what Ginger or Murray scripted for themselves when they were young, in love, and planning their future in Toronto. But it is where they finally settled and over the course of some 30-odd years, established roots and supported their remaining four children out the door.

Some highway near Lake Huron, circa 1960

It was a unique treat for the family. Two days of frolicking at a cottage, swimming in the lake, sand between toes, sleeping in a different bed, and snacks. The musty old smell of wood and unpolished furnishings reminded me I was not at home. Cold at night. Warm during the day. Mom even washed my hair as I sat on a raft in the water. Now driving home, the sun, sand, and fresh air worked their magic as I lay my tired head on my crossed arms, resting on the front seat bench. I looked ahead at the pavement as it raced under the front of the car. The centre line seemed to come and go faster and faster. The road seemed to raise up and then down again. Up and then down again.

Oh oh.

That awful but familiar feeling crept into my brain. I felt fuzzy and my stomach turned flip flops. I felt awful, but before I could say a word, out it came.

Oh, it tastes awful and there is so much of it. Orange juice and toast from breakfast.

Now Dad is yelling, and Mom turns around to look at me. She rolls her eyes but puts her cool hand on my forehead saying, "Oh, Kim."

The car stops. Dad is standing on the side of the road with Miles as Mom cleans up.

"Look at that, Miles," Dad says, waving his arm at the passing vehicles. "All those other Dads driving home, and here I am. Afraid to put my hands in my dang pockets."

Dad used to tell this story of our memorable cottage visit often. Although my upheaval was the most dramatic, in fact, I was not the only one to get sick on that holiday. I just waited until we were in the car.

Dad often had a knack for seeing the humour. After five children, it may have been easier, or it was the only thing one could do.

Toronto, circa 1965

I know that summer is almost over when I hear advertising for the CNE - the Canadian National Exhibition held annually at the fairgrounds in Toronto. We went frequently when older, but it was also an event that mom took us to as kids.

I am sitting on a stool next to mom under the Bingo Tent. I am trying to keep up with the caller and almost miss the win.

"Bingo," Mom yells, pointing at my card.

"Bingo," I repeat.

"What prize would you like?" the carnival worker asks me.

"Mom, can we get the bird?" I spy a cute budgie in a cage.

"No."

"Please."

"No, I am not carrying that bird while you go on the rides."

Hmm. I want to go on rides.

I don't recall ever challenging the fact that mom happily carried the personal hair dryer while we went on the rides.

But she used that prize in our home for years. It included a

plastic bonnet that fit over your head with a large tube leading to the fan and motor housing.

< Mom under the hair dryer that eventually replaced the one I won at the CNE. At the kitchen table in Listowel.

Listowel, circa 1966

Waking late, I look across the room to the other twin bed and see it is empty, already made. I go downstairs to the kitchen, surprised when I see my former elementary school teacher, Elaine Bodkin, (Miss Bodkin to me) sitting at the kitchen table with Mom. I knew she had driven from the Chatham area to visit the family. I had shared my room with her, but I had thought she would leave early that morning.

"Don't you remember last night?" she asked with a smile.

No. I didn't recall that she had to waken me through the night to get my mother. Turns out Miss Bodkin was ill and needed help. She had to stay for a while longer. I guess I went back to sleep and didn't retain the night's upset.

This friendship with our elementary teacher from Vincent Massey Public School continued for years, and I think of it when I consider how welcoming my parents were to others. Their home was open to friends of their kids, and even teachers. Miss Bodkin had a soft spot for Miles and kept in touch with him, even after our parents died.

Mom had a knack for treating people in a way that put them at ease. She told me a sign of class was the ability to treat another person the same, regardless of their perceived position in society.

A minister's wife was among the visitors one night in our home and mom quietly approached her, as she had the others, to offer her a drink. Years later, this woman told me,

"Your mom didn't make a big fuss about it, like some would do, saying things like, 'I guess you don't want a real drink, eh?' and creating such a public display that I would feel compelled to ask for something else. She just asked quietly what I would like, and she brought me my drink."

Listowel, circa 1967

Our next-door neighbour Jack was running up our back porch steps taking them two at a time. "I've got three. I've got three," he shouted. He was equally stunned and over-the-moon about the birth of triplets, unexpected until in the delivery room. The joy was followed by sorrow when Jack and Ev lost two of the babies. Years later I learned that as they grieved and learned to care for a very tiny baby boy at home, it was Mom who went in to help, doing laundry and housework. No fanfare. Just a good friend doing what she could.

Listowel, circa 1967

Miles and Jan have a hold of Mom by her arms in a kitchen chair while Bill straps the roller skates onto her stockinged feet. She is wearing her usual housedress, and as Bill ties his skates on her feet, the boys are giddy thinking of their prim mother in roller skates.

She is protesting, but she is laughing too. There's no real

strong-arming here.

The boys help her stand, and she stretches her arms out as a balancing rod. The laughs continue as the prank builds.

They move the table, and Bill walks to the other side of the room.

"Ok guys, send her over. Mom. You can do this."

"No, no, you brats," she calls between laughs, just a little nervous about what is coming, thinking perhaps they won't carry it that far.

But Jan and Miles give her a little shove, and Mom sails across four feet of linoleum floor, her laughter now tinged with a few yelps of fear.

Bill catches her by her outstretched arms, steadies her, and then, with another gentle shove, returns her backwards.

And back and forth she goes a couple more times until she has to confess what all the laughter has done to a bladder weakened by five pregnancies.

Showing no mercy, they put her out on the side porch and call neighbour and good friend Evelyn Reis, who can look out her kitchen window and see the side porch.

"Look out your kitchen window, Ev. Our mother peed herself."

Listowel, circa 1970

Mom lifts the Sears Winter Catalogue off the sideboard and beckons me. She brings out the wallpaper we selected for my bedroom; we need to find a new bedspread. The big orange and brown floral pattern with bedspread and matching curtains will contrast nicely with the green stripped paper, we agree. Anything but girly pink, I plead.

Mom is ready to decorate again.

My bedroom was an easier task than the front hall, which

rose to 20 feet in height in sections. Dad forbade her from climbing the scaffolding they had created with ladders and boards over the curving 18-step staircase. He climbed up to apply the first roll and promptly put his fist through it.

Mom forbade him from helping and completed the task. The paper lasted and was not replaced in the years that followed.

Decorating was a favourite pastime of Mom's. A family wedding sometimes prompted new carpets and drapes in the living room and dining room. Fresh paint would be applied to the baseboards or the kitchen cupboards regularly. She liked to experiment with paint and wallpaper.

A favourite memory is of her standing on a ladder, paintbrush in hand, her hair tied back in a kerchief. When prompted, she would stick out her tongue and cross her eyes, giving us what she called the "Double Whammy" and making us laugh.

Listowel, circa 1970s

Dad and I are sitting on the back steps of our home in Listowel. I'm not sure why we are there, but I know it was warm and sunny.

I am watching the ants as they scurry across the sidewalk, and I lift my foot and bring it down on one.

"Kim. Why did you do that?" Dad asked. "That little ant wasn't hurting you. He was just busy going about his life. He had a right to live."

My father denied any spiritual or religious reasoning in his logic, just a deep respect for all living things. But 'all God's creatures' comes to mind when I reflect on this memory.

I still hate stepping on ants!

Summer, circa 1970s

"If there's a God I heaven, he sure blew this one." My father vehemently expressed his outrage at hearing about the death of a mother of eight children. She was a minister's wife in town, and someone I had come to know through babysitting. She always spent time at the door with me before I left, sharing her wisdom, and giving me some adult attention.

I had arrived home, devastated by the news.

A religion, or faith in a higher power, was not observed in our home. We could attend church with friends if we wanted, but as he aged, Dad claimed to be agnostic and then became firmly atheist. He referred to religion as a "nice crutch," but it's one I wish he had relied on as he faced his own death.

Bill described him as iconoclastic, defined by Oxford as "someone who criticizes popular beliefs or established customs and ideas." (Leave it to Bill to use a word I had to look up!)

Dad told me that Jesus taught a good way to live, and as Jan reflected, Dad **lived** the Golden Rule. But faith was one of the roots Lydia planted that Murray eventually cut.

Christmas, circa 1980s

"Yes, I made it," Dad said, beaming.

"It" was a sturdy, four-leg table, made of blonde wood and covered in urethane to protect the surface. One for me, and one for Bev. In his retirement, Dad had resurrected his table saw and made these for us. Mine could hold my typewriter and hers a sewing machine, he suggested. He laughed, and his eyes twinkled mischievously as he added, "Someday you will want to throw this out, but you'll say, 'I can't do that, Dad made it.'"

Over the years, the table has served many purposes, including a bar, a buffet table, and a television stand. No typewriter, but it held my computer and was my writing centre as I struggled to earn a Master of Arts in my 50s. Now it holds my sewing machine. But he was right-this table will go to the nursing home with me. I can't throw it out. Dad made it.

In the news, 1980

If Dad had some rocky years at Campbell Soup, you would never know it by the accolades he received when he retired in 1980, just shy of 45 years after he started at the Toronto plant.

A formal dinner with a "roasting" was attended by colleagues from both Listowel and Toronto. The Listowel Banner captured a photo of him leaving the plant for the last time, and in the accompanying story noted that he had been walking the two miles to and from work every day for a few years. I recall the anxiety he put us through the night he did the walk in a severe winter storm, the kind of storm in which farmers were known to lose their way from house to barn because the visibility is so poor. He admitted when he came in the door that he should not have walked that day! But he took to heart the advice the company doctor gave him to start walking, and he continued walking after retirement, about town and at the golf course.

Dad was mostly an arm-chair athlete. A weekly Saturday night battle pitted a movie for me vs the hockey game for him. He usually won. But, he loved his golf, and I often caddied for him when I was younger. In his retirement, he took full advantage of the time and was well-known at the local club. First one on the course in spring and last one off in fall. We teased him that he ran, not walked, after the ball.

Despite his pleas, mom would not join him. Her preference for activity was an in-door sport that took her away from the house as often as three times a week when I was younger, and she got her own fair share of press because of her success.

Miles and Kim tap dancing in Chatham. Mom looking sharp in pinstripes and hat. She dressed this way for the trip home after major surgery. Typical family scene at the kitchen table in Listowel with numerous cups of Mom's coffee: Dad reading while others talk.

Christmas dinner in Listowel. Likely the year when Bill was touring Europe as Aunt Peg is in his usual seat next to Dad. Miles, Kim, and Rick on the left. On the right, Uncle Ray, Jan, Aunt Bette, and Sharon's husband John. That's fruit salad in the dishes, always served as a starter. Next photo is of Mom bringing the Christmas pudding to the table at another Christmas. Jim and Bill at the table.

1977, back: Miles holding new-born Laura, Jim, Jan, Rick, Bill. Centre: Kim, Kathy, Dad, Mom, Bev, Linda, and front: Scott, Shannon, Sean, and Sarah. 1986, on the front porch. Back row: Bev, Kim, Dad, Mom, Shannon; next row: Bill, Laura, Amy, Sean, Sarah, Linda; front row: Jim with Mark, Miles, and Rick.

Chapter 35

Strike

April 23, 1944
My Darling Ginger: …When we were up this morning, we dropped
our bombs early and went for a side-up through the clouds. We met a
Harvard and chased it around for a while. I only have three or four
more trips to make before I am finished… I will close now Hon. Don't
work too hard at your new job… Remember that I still love you and
always will. So long for now Sweetheart. I'll write again to-morrow
night. I love you and miss you. Good-night Darling, Murray.

Ginger

In a Canadian family with four boys, one might expect the
house to be cluttered with sports equipment such as hockey
sticks, soccer balls, or baseball bats; they might fill the
clothesline with team jerseys or airing out athletic footwear,
weekend schedules taken over by tournaments and weekdays
filled with practices.

And while Dad was an avid golfer in later years, the award-
winning athlete in our family was not to be found among the
males.

The person who pursued a passion several times a week,
entered weekend tournaments, brought home enough

hardware to spill out of the china cabinet, and gave Dad a coaching role was Mom.

The sport was bowling! The Canadian game of 5-pin bowling to be exact.

Her gear included her own bowling shoes, kept in a bowling bag, and in later years, her own monogrammed bowling balls. And, of course, a team shirt, or several team shirts as she bowled three nights a week when I was young.

When exactly she began to bowl, I am not sure, but in Listowel with Dad working the afternoon shift, she bowled Monday, Wednesday, and Friday nights. Bill or Jan was usually in charge on the weeknights, but on Friday nights, when they had part-time jobs, she occasionally left Miles and I on our own with the promise to bring back a treat. We could have a pop, or we could have chips, not both.

Over the years, she collected some serious hardware, and she developed her own social circle; it was one way she managed her depression and the loneliness she felt with Dad gone every evening.

Bowling Alleys, like all sports, evolved their own culture. Most small-town lanes in the 60s included a snack bar and were a source of employment for local youth. Larger city lanes sometimes offered a bar service, but not Listowel.

In the early years, the Listowel Lanes still employed pin boys. They sat up on a ledge, out of sight behind the pins, and it was their job to remove toppled pins out of the way and reset after three balls. They had to follow the play, so they knew when to reset. If someone got a spare, for instance, they needed to know that it required a second reset after only one ball. Sometimes you could see their legs dangling down and when someone threw an aggressive ball, you saw them quickly snatch their legs back up and out of the way of flying pins. Bowlers would also hear the occasional holler-this was a small town, and the pin boys were not strangers; they were known to the players. Eventually the Listowel Lanes installed modern, automatic lanes, although you still had to learn how to count and keep score. That technology came later.

Mom had her own style, and it included her attire. It was a part of her secret sauce. She didn't wear slacks; instead, she wore bowling skirts. In the earlier years, skirts were a tournament requirement, so her strategy was to always wear tournament-approved clothing. She felt it gave her an edge when she was comfortable wearing the required clothing. Not unlike the lucky shirt or memorable hair cut you see athletes employ.

One of her bowling skirts was a grey wool, midi-length A-line. I found it in her closet when I was in high school when the midi skirt was 'in.' I paired it with a red turtleneck and wore my hair up in a bun, as Dad called it, my off-the-konk hairstyle. When I wore that skirt and sweater, I felt like I was 'cool.' Someone at school asked with admiration.

"Kim, where did you get the skirt?"

It was one of those few times when I had the wits to respond in the right way. *"Oh, some shop in Toronto,"* I said nonchalantly. *"Wow,"* she responded. We considered anything from Toronto to be a winner in our rural, small-town circles. No doubt Mom purchased the skirt in Toronto, but a fellow student didn't need to know I got it out of my mother's closet.

5-pin bowling was a Canadian invention, launched in 1909 in Toronto when customers complained to Thomas F. Ryan about the weight of the 10-pin balls. It opened the sport to children, and I was one of them.

Along with my good friend Janet, I went to the Listowel Lanes
every Saturday morning, where John and Kay Duke ran a very
active children's league. We were about 9 years old. Of course,
the highlight was buying a treat afterward. We thought we were
funny walking home in the winter with ice-cream cones. If we
were lucky, we got a quarter from our parents to spend the
afternoon at the movies. I still remember John Wayne saying
"damn" in a movie and being shocked.

Mom entered lots of bowling tournaments held in different
cities across Ontario. Dad drove so she didn't have to, and he
boasted about looking after her. He mixed her the rum and 7-up
she enjoyed but made sure her alcohol intake didn't interfere
with her game!

"Just one drink to energize her when she starts to slump," is
how he detailed his coaching strategy.

< Listowel Banner clipping with
Ernie Webb, Mom, Jean Cooper,
and Kay Duke entered in the
Carling Eastern Canada
Competition. (Listowel Banner)

FOUR LOCAL BOWLERS will be entered as part of a team from this zone in the Carling Eastern Canada Championships to be held in Scarborough March 30 to April 1. Taking part will be, from left, Ernie Webb, Ginger Dadson, Jean Cooper and Kay Duke, Mr. Webb is also the new owner of the Listowel bowling lanes. (Banner Photo)

He enjoyed teasing her and, after winning one tournament,
referred to her as the Queen of the Lanes.

She entered a popular television show produced by CKCO
Television in the 70s and 80s called Bowling for Dollars. Bowlers
tried to roll three strikes in a row for a pot of money that
increased each week it was not won. Winners shared the pot
with a so-called Pin-Pal, a name pulled out of a drum.

They taped the show at Twin City Bowl in Kitchener, and like all reality shows, Mom signed a confidentiality agreement that prevented her from telling how she did until after the show aired.

I still remember the excitement and anticipation as we sat down to watch Mom on our old black and white Zenith television.

We watched her choose a ball and walk to the centre dot mid-way down her lane, aligning herself by placing her right foot forward slightly. With elbows bent, she held her ball up, about chin height, the ball in her right hand and her left hand resting lightly on top of it. Her face was a mask of concentration, focused on the lane markings further down the alley between the gutters. Her eyes flickered between the markings and the pins. At just the right moment, she moved forward, raising the ball. Her right arm began to swing back, ball still in hand, as she continued forward, and then, as she returned her arm to the front, she released the ball. It landed softly on the alley just past the foul line. She kept her right arm outstretched, straight, as though she willed the ball to the right spot, as her right leg ended up crossing the back of her slightly bent left leg. Toe tips back of the foul line. It's the follow-through I recognized from her coaching me in this sport.

All the pins fell. Strike 1. We cheered.

The second set up began, just like the first, and we watched again the perfect execution, the follow-through at the end.

And again, all pins fell. Strike 2. We cheered even louder.

Now we were nervous, as no doubt she was at the time. She set up and executed again. Our eyes followed the ball, and our shoulders drooped. Pins were left standing. We turned to look at Mom, and she was laughing.

She was still our favourite—albeit only—athlete of the family!

Chapter 36

Perfectly Imperfect Part I

March 14, 1944
My dear Ginger … Try not to miss me so much, for we will not be seeing much of each other until this whole course is over. Have you got any coal left in the cellar? Don't forget you will have to pay for the next delivery. I will be able to send you some money at the end of the month… Good night and kisses to you both. Murray.

Dad and Mom

It's only when someone has children of their own that they can begin to put their childhood experiences into perspective. I remember worrying about doing what was best for my children, particularly when I went back to work. A piece of wisdom came to me from a Mennonite neighbour who told me my children would only know what they know. I loved them and cared for them. We would be fine. She was right. When I think of my own parents, whatever missteps they may have made in their child-rearing choices, we all knew they loved us. I knew a father who said those words out loud, and a mother who expressed it in practical ways. We were all spoiled, if only because they loved us.

With no handbook delivered alongside the baby, parents bring their own life experience to this daunting task of raising the next generation. Thus, the father that my eldest brother Rick described from his youth, and the one I, as the fifth and youngest child knew, differed.

Rick was the firstborn, with all the inherent hopes and dreams focused on him for six years before any other children arrived. Dad was away for some of this time, serving in the RCAF. On his return, he was building his career, earning positions of more authority at work, and accepting transfers. Rick remembered a father who was tough in expectations and angry with perceived shortcomings. I suspect Dad was likely tougher on himself as well, afraid the plans he and Mom had made were falling behind because of the war. Patience was thin. Second-born Bill described Dad as driven.

I was the last born, growing up in a rural town with a father who had nothing to prove. He had already experienced the highs and lows of his career and knew what he would do with them.

Dad grew in wisdom from the experience at Campbell Soup, in part because of the solid foundation that Fred and Lydia had given him. It didn't come easy, as evidenced by the small kitchen table flying across the backyard in Chatham. I know now that incident happened when issues at work were building toward untenable.

The 15 years between the first and the fifth born were also filled with parenting experience. Both Mom and Dad claimed experience was a brilliant teacher. Mom told me it horrified her that she had followed trending advice when Bill was young, to put his dinner into the refrigerator and serve it for breakfast if he didn't eat it.

In contrast to Rick's memories, I knew a father who had a temper, but who could also bring calm and discussion to a situation. I once repeated a joke I had heard older kids laugh at, and I wanted to make Dad laugh. That would be a big deal to an 11-year-old wanting to look mature. But the joke contained a word that starts with 'f,' and when it came out of my mouth, Dad exploded. The next thing I knew, I was upstairs in bed, crying, not sure what I had done wrong. He came upstairs after a while. "Do you know what the word means?" He calmly explained his anger, and said I was to never use that word again. I had never heard the word before, did not know its meaning, and it still makes me uncomfortable. Such is the power that parents yield.

Dad could also take a joke at his own expense. Bill told a story about overhearing Dad chastise teenaged Miles; when Dad finished with the lecture, Miles looked at him and said in a serious tone of voice, "You know Murray, we can't be friends after this." Dad just broke down and laughed.

Good humour was his reaction to my infamous party held after a school dance. Who knew so many would come after I called, "Party at Dadson's" out the car window on my way home? It was a Friday night, and I knew my parents were at home. This was something I failed to mention to my peers. As people showed up, I told those who had brought beer I couldn't let them into the house. I was underage. An alley ran behind our home, a perfect gathering place for kids, so some of the party moved there. Music followed. Dad was chatting with a bunch of kids on the front porch. Mom was fretting upstairs in their bedroom. It wasn't long before a neighbour called the police. (Or maybe my parents did!) My friend Nancy hid in the neighbour's doghouse in their garage as the police officer walked by with a flashlight. Debbie left just before her police officer father showed up. Dad was in the alley when a young officer picked up an empty bottle of beer, exclaiming, "Look what I found. An empty beer bottle." Dad picked up another bottle and exclaimed in response, "And look what I found, a full one!" The police had the intended effect, and everyone fled. Much to my relief. Dad just never let me forget it. "Kim really knows how to throw a party, eh?" No one had to tell me I had made a mistake and not to do it again.

Dad saw these episodes as the lessons they were; when Miles came home one night with a black eye, Dad just advised steak and listened as Miles told him life wasn't a bowl of cherries. He had been targeted because he had refused to fight.

Mom also brought a sense of humour to her role, although not so much about parties or black eyes. When she complained she was not running a restaurant when someone didn't like what she served, the artists in the family designed a five-foot-long sign that was tacked high on the kitchen wall reading: Ginger's Kitchen. The marquee stayed up for a long time.

One wintry evening, Miles showed up on his snowmobile. He came into the house and climbed the stairs to get Mom out of bed and (still in nightgown) into a snowmobile suit. Between laughs and weak protests, he provided her with boots and then lead her outside for a quick ride.

Regardless of his negative memories, Rick valued family and made sure his children knew their grandparents. For years, they always made the 10 to 12-hour car trip to Listowel to spend Christmas with us, four children and gifts packed into the car. On one memorable trip, they arrived in Listowel in the middle of the night, a good time to travel with young ones as they sleep. However, it raised the suspicions of a police officer who stopped them. He aimed his flashlight into the back of the van, where it highlighted four sleeping children. He quietly backed away from the van, apologizing in a whispered voice. We all loved when Rick and his family came home, especially when the children were babies who would be passed around from one set of loving arms to another. I remember seeing my brother Jan holding one of the babies in his arms while they were alone in the family room. He was cooing and blowing raspberries on the baby's tummy. Loving babies is in the Dadson genes, I think.

But we also knew Dad could exhibit a short temper when provoked. One provocation would be if we disrespected our mother, which I did as a teenager, only to discover the consequences were swift and harsh. Showing respect was an important value, as Miles discovered after he flippantly said someone had "kicked the bucket" as we passed a funeral home. Dad's rebuke was fast and furious.

Another provocation would be if we behaved as though we were better than someone else. I said something demeaning about another person, and my father berated me: "Who do you think you are?" His words still ring in my head, his disappointment like a sharp slap. He would get upset if he perceived an injustice or if someone acted as though they were superior to others. Two brothers described Dad as honest, to a fault, according to Jan, or to the point of being blunt, according to Bill.

The fact I was the only girl also played into what we experienced. It shocked me to learn that when Miles left Listowel to get work, Dad drove him to the edge of town in the morning, dropped him off and said, "Good luck." Miles hitchhiked into Kitchener, and by that afternoon, he had a job and found a place to live. Conversely, when my date's car broke down in Kitchener, my parents drove the hour to pick me up. While it relieved me when they came to get me, as I knew they would, they were strict with me. The only time Dad said anything about my dating was when I had plans to go to the drive-in, concerned because my brothers referred to it as the "passion pit." I convinced him it was okay.

Dad, frequently in his absent-minded professor role, could be oblivious of his children's projects, even when they were suspect. Jan tells the story of stealing lumber from behind a business and building a raft for the creek that ran at the bottom of O'Brien Drive, in Chatham.

"Dad came home and saw us hammering and noted we were busy creating something. He just said, 'good for you kids' or something like that. He never questioned where the lumber came from."

Dad was afforded this luxury because Mom was the main disciplinarian. While work was one distraction, he also knew Mom had his back. She could count on him as well. My parents had different parenting styles, but one thing we all knew for sure: they talked to each other. There was no putting one over the other because they always had each other's backs.

But the fact remained, Mom was the one who handled most of the child rearing, and this duty only increased when Dad was relegated to the afternoon shift after the move to Listowel.

Chapter 37

Perfectly Imperfect Part II

Thursday, Mar. 16, 1944
Dear Ginger: –... I did not write last night Hon, but phoned instead. It sure was nice to hear your voice. Your mail seems to be coming into me regularly now Sweetheart. Keep the good work up. The letter I got this morning was written on Tuesday night... Loads of kisses & all my love, Murray.

Mom and Dad

After his customary lunch of eggs and bacon, and their daily game of cribbage, Dad left the house each weekday by 2 p.m. and didn't return until midnight. It was up to Mom to deal with any issues after school and evenings. Incidents such as finding cigarettes in my bedroom drawer. Or when the boys wrestled on the living room floor. It began as a joke, but as testosterone levels increased, there was always the moment it turned serious. Mom pleaded with them to stop. On at least one occasion, I recall her resorting to tears.

Rick's friend from high school days in Toronto offered a different perspective of our parents. John Wheatley said he envied the fact Rick was allowed to have a car. No doubt Dad recalled the car his mother arranged for him and his brothers at the same age. John described our mother as harried and how she would permit him and Rick to take me out when I was two years old.

What John didn't know was what managing a household with a 17-year-old teenager at one end, three busy boys aged 11, 8, and 6 in the middle, and a two-year-old at the other end could encompass. She was busy!

In one escapade, Jan unwittingly pulled cupboards right off the kitchen wall as he tried climbing them to get a box of chalk. It was stored in the cupboard above the stove and Jan had kneeled on the stove to reach the cupboards. Mom and Dad were out, and Rick was sitting. Rick just observed the mess and told Jan to clean it up. He picked up the cans of food that came crashing onto the floor, lining them up on the table and chairs. And he swept the chalk that was now chalk dust.

In another incident, Bill pushed Miles and Jan on a toboggan down a set of stairs attached to a cloverleaf over the QEW. It was a great ride until the end when they toppled, and both ended up with fat lips.

One day Miles got separated from Mom in a store-the specific details are lost in time-but the store was on the other side of the QEW from our home. He remembers sitting on a patch of grass and contemplating how to cross the highway when the police picked him up. They brought him home, and as they left, they called over their loudspeaker: "Don't get lost again, Milesy."

When we were ill, it was Mom who kept vigil. All night with Jan, after he flew over the handlebars of a bike, hitting his head on the cement. When I was ill, there was nothing more comforting than the sound of Mom moving about the house, doing chores. Her cool hand on my fevered forehead brought comfort when she paused by my bed, ginger-ale in hand. When I was recovering, she would run a hot bath. On my return to bed, I discovered clean sheets that carried the fresh smell of the outdoors throughout the room. Bliss!

Mom had a sixth sense about her kids, like the night she checked in on Miles after bedtime to discover a thin, red line running up the inside of his arm, a classic sign of blood poisoning. They rushed him to the hospital. The backyard fort he had built came down. The poisoning was likely the result of a bug bite from an insect in the mattress that had been pulled out of a neighbour's garage attic.

Mom had strict rules; a point of pride for her was that she could take her young brood into a restaurant, and they would behave. This was important, especially around the times we moved. As a family, we didn't dine out that often, but we lived in hotels and ate in restaurants while we waited for more than one house to be ready for us when we moved. Our vacations to the U.S. usually included some eating out while on the road. It was a time for chocolate milk and choosing songs on the mini table-top juke box. 'Soldier Boy' by the Shirelles was one of my favourites.

Mom had a look that meant business if challenged, as Miles discovered the time he said "no" to her request he take a laundry basket upstairs. The scenario repeated some 40 years later during a visit, and he teased her, refusing the request. She looked, but he told her that "the look" wouldn't work anymore, and they shared a laugh. Of course, he took the basket up the stairs.

I played at a friend's home where the living room was off limits to the kids. In contrast, our home wasn't an artificial show piece. We lived in it. And it was open to our friends, but Mom was no pushover. When Bill's classmate ended up on the street after his parents split, she welcomed the teenager in. As Dow moved clothes in through the back door, she stood on the landing and told him he must obey the rules of the house, including curfew. "Yes, Mrs. D.," he smiled.

The welcome mat continued even after we left home. After Bill moved to Hamilton, he invited an English couple, who had just arrived in Canada, to our home for Christmas. He knew he could count on Mom to be a generous host. She made sure there were gifts under the tree and a place at the table for them.

I now realize the energy and effort it took for her to keep a large four-bedroom home, with four-plus kids and their friends coming and going, organized, and cleaned.

Mom's job was to manage the home front, including "the books" she kept with precision each month, carefully noting all household bills. In fact, the "conversation" we had before I married involved how to keep the books along with her advice that I should retain the management of this task. Control of the purse strings.

I regret that the messages of the women's movement belittled how she saw her work at home. My parents' marriage was a partnership in every sense of the word. She juggled Dad's pay and supported our requests when she could or snipped where needed to make it work. When Rick expected airfare to come home from university, she sent him bus fare. We often joked that Mom owned shares in Simpson Sears, as it was her credit card that allowed her to dress us in a manner she desired (aka no jeans).

She dealt with a lot, from kitchen cupboards flying off the

wall, to the more innocent when Miles and Jan took slabs of rocks in a wagon to the bank because it had flecks of what they believed was gold. Some scared her, such as Jan's bicycle accident, or the time I got into a mix of medications. It was Mom we all talked to or turned to when life presented challenges.

Mom came to our defense if needed, berating a teacher who told Miles he should quit school. She believed us, calling the police when my girlfriends and I, around age 10, told her about an older man in the neighbourhood who paid too much attention to me. She supported our dreams, such as Rick's to attend university in the United States and Bill's to leave university for travel through Europe. She was there after the birth of my first child and didn't laugh at me when I asked, in all seriousness, if she would keep an eye on him while I showered.

Mom was there if we needed to talk, whether at the kitchen table late into the evening, in the bathroom while she put on her make-up, or on the phone in later years. She sacrificed much and provided the best counsel she knew how.

Mom told me she and Dad wanted their children "to stand on their own two feet," a message I was to find later that I took seriously. They enabled our dreams by supporting what education or life experiences they believed would get us to where we were headed. They loved us, sometimes not making the best choices for us, but doing their utmost based on their own experiences.

Our parents were perfectly imperfect as they loved us into adulthood, although according to mom, her biggest challenge came with her fifth child.

Chapter 38

Mothers and Daughters

March 31, 1944
My dear Ginger… Gosh, I wish you were home when I phoned a while ago. I wanted to hear your voice. I feel down in the dumps to-day. I guess the weather has something to do with it too. But the weather will surely break soon; and then everything will seem brighter. I really have so much to be thankful for, I shouldn't be feeling blue… Yours always, Murray

Ginger and Kim

I was the lone daughter in the family, following four boys. I must have felt outnumbered as I frequently asked my parents for a sister, so much so they thought about adopting. Perhaps their experience of raising a girl dissuaded them from the idea.

My mother always told me I was more work than my four brothers - combined. Sometimes she said it with a smile. I can't say I was entirely displeased at this recognition that I had some spunk or courage in me. At least that's how I interpreted her comment. It has served me well over the years as I pursued different careers and raised my family.

My status as the youngest has also shaped me, because I had

older siblings by which to measure my progress. The need to catch up, grow up, and be on the move was always strong within me.

For instance, when I was a toddler, it was common practice to keep children confined in wooden playpens. It kept them safe

and presumably in one spot. However, I was able to move my playpen from the backyard to the front yard by putting my legs through the bars and pushing.

< *The author, unhappy in her playpen.*

My parents thought they had a fix for the problem when they removed the wheels.

Apparently not.

I put my legs out between the bars and with a firm grasp on the bars with my hands, I humped my way around the house. If not a demonstration of my strength, it was, I believe, an ingenious scientific calculation on my behalf. My mother likely didn't think so when the neighbours laughed.

When I reflect on this oft-repeated story, which served as an example of the trouble I could cause, I think it makes sense given the context of the times and of our home. Determined girls were trouble, while determined boys were, well, determined.

Ok, I was the instigator of two fires, one involving a bedroom lamp (with Miles as my accomplice-Mom's hat looked so pretty on the lamp with the light on) and another in the oven with my plastic play dishes (Mom didn't know they were in the oven when she turned it on). I was also the one who climbed out of the crib and ate a bunch of pills that were in bottles on top of the nearby dresser. The family still went on the planned trip into the U.S. after checking with the doctor. I was told I bounced on the motel bed "all night," still high, much to my mother's dismay.

As Mom's letter to my father hinted when I was born, (*And I'll bet she will be spoilt. We will have to watch ourselves.)* my parents were on guard against special treatment. In many ways, I think they accomplished that. On the other hand, they were both simultaneously more relaxed with four children under the belt, so to speak, and over-protective with a girl this time round.

Like all younger siblings, if I saw the boys allowed to do things I could not, I protested loudly, while Mom tried her best to create a girly girl. Like many little girls, I took pleasure in the crinolines and fancy dresses, if not the directions to be quiet or demure. I played with dolls by creating stories, such as being a single working woman with my Barbie doll and her furniture fashioned out of old tissue boxes. But there came a time when I resisted childish ways and tried to exert opinions that were in opposition to what Mom thought. It often resulted in battles between us which intensified when I entered my teens. On one rare occasion, Dad told her to leave me alone.

It was a huge win when my sister-in-law Linda on one visit came to me and said, "Kimmy, go get your skirts. I talked your mother into one inch, and I will help you hem them." Here, finally, was the sister that I had begged my parents for all those years ago.

The relationship between Mom and I evolved as I matured, although the ability to irritate each other was never really gone. When Mom was dying, I sat next to her one day and tried to communicate an acknowledgment of what I put her through.

"I can appreciate what you did for me now that I have children."

Instead of the heart-to-heart about the trials of being a mother I was hoping for, I got a lecture about my parenting.

Sometimes she didn't pull any punches, whether or not we needed it.

The male influence in our household was strong. The tolerance level for emotional outbursts or creating drama was low. I had a minor meltdown at one point as we planned my wedding. It had nothing to do with her, but everything to do with feeling overwhelmed. Mom had no patience to tolerate the outburst, telling me to "stop it." She had strong common sense and would scold me for "wearing your heart on your sleeve" if I got too emotional. As I matured, I was happy in my femininity and what made me different from my brothers. Make up. Check. Wearing a dress. Check. I could have a baby someday. Check. Check.

But the idea that as a woman I was somehow the 'weaker sex' without autonomy, was reinforced by both society and at home. It was long a sore point, as illustrated with this story and its impact.

Summer, 1978

"I am so glad you are marrying Jim. Dad and I have looked after you all these years, and now Jim will look after you," my mother announced.

< Mom and me on my wedding day.

It was a warm summer's day, the kind where you just feel good about being alive. Mom and I were in the car traveling along the highway that connected our small town to another, the journey running past family farms boasting painted barns, Holsteins munching in pastures, and fields of ripening corn and golden wheat dancing in the breeze. We were on our way to check out the flowers for my upcoming wedding.

"You mean I have never been responsible for myself?" I asked, incredulous. Ready to laugh at the idea, I was brought up short when without missing a beat she responded in all seriousness: "No."

As stubborn or strong-willed as I was, Mom's words and opinions remained important to me. So, just like that, the past year in which I lived on my own, paid rent, purchased groceries, budgeted for that new dress, and became master of my domain (in other words stood on my own two feet) evaporated. My year of proving I could support myself hadn't even registered with her.

According to my mother, I had not been responsible for myself in the past year, or in the three previous years when I lived in Toronto attending school.

The past year of working fulltime was an important milestone for me. Perhaps I compared this accomplishment to my mother's story of her paycheque supporting her parents. That made her an adult, in her eyes. I equated attaining adulthood with earning a paycheque and not relying on my parents.

After graduation from Ryerson, I deliberately held off on marriage to prove I could support myself. I didn't want to enter marriage with the old-fashioned notion I needed a husband to be complete or to support me.

Instead, I focused my efforts toward finding a job. I sent out applications across the province, prepared to move away to begin this next chapter. If my search brought me back to Listowel, I told Mom I would get an apartment rather than live at home. "Why?" she had asked, hurt. I needed to prove that I could support myself before I married, I explained.

"You are too independent," she told me.

How we measured or viewed the milestones in our lives was vastly different. Mom thought her life began the day she married Dad. I sought autonomy.

As it was, I landed a job in Wingham, a small town down the road from Listowel. Commuting was out of the question as I didn't own a car, so I got my wish to look for my own place away from home. (Amazingly, I was hired despite this lack of a vehicle. The publisher's car would be available for out-of-town assignments, and I recognize the irony of thinking I was independent while living in a rural area without transportation!)

My first apartment was in a cinderblock building behind main street businesses, and it didn't come close to Mary Tyler Moore's stylish abode in the TV show that inspired me in the 70s.

When you entered my apartment, you were in the kitchen. There was just enough space to walk between the refrigerator and the table. If you opened the fridge door or pulled out a chair to sit, there wasn't room to walk. The adjoining living room had lots of natural light thanks to a large picture window. It helped the space from being completely cheerless. The extra-long cord on the telephone reached every room, from the bedroom, across the living room, and into the bathroom.

The apartment was not spacious or fancy, but it was mine.

My brother Rick visited bearing three gifts: a water pitcher with matching glasses, cleanser with a scrub pad he used to clean the rust stain in the bathtub, and a peephole for the door! On previous visits home, he would tell Mom to cut the apron strings where I was concerned, and I would get defensive at what I saw as a comment on my shortcomings. With these gifts, this big brother was supporting my newfound independence, and I appreciated both the help with the bathtub and the peephole which provided a measure of security.

I managed the money I earned as a reporter at the town's weekly newspaper. I walked to work every day and began to learn what it means to have a professional life and colleagues. I succeeded in convincing a municipal council to trust my reporting abilities, I challenged a local club when it balked at having a female reporter attend an event, and I began to get to know the community.

I was responsible and standing on my own two feet, an accomplishment I thought would meet Mom's criteria.

Then came the conversation in the car where her words undercut my achievement. They remained an undercurrent in my life that neither of us could have foreseen.

If you had asked me at the time of our conversation, I would have retorted of course, I didn't believe her. I had even laughed about it over the years. But some 30 years later, this conversation came back to haunt me in a counselling session. My mother's comment had deeply impacted me.

Her approach to parenting had always been to exert control. That was her definition of looking after me. Now she was suggesting this control was being passed to my husband.

Mom had always directed many aspects of my life, from clothing choices to hair styles. When I was in elementary school, she put out the clothes I would wear each day. She permed my hair to manage the style she preferred. She didn't push me out to get part-time jobs when I was a teen, recognizing that when I had money, I could make my own decisions about some things. I was eager to earn my own money and had a thriving babysitting business as well as the usual part-time jobs in retail. I recall her look of shock when I announced one afternoon that I had signed up for a school sponsored trip to Spain, paid for with the babysitting money in my bank account.

As I grew and asserted my opinions, she belittled my choices.

Your skirt is too short.

Your hair is too long.

You need to lose weight.

You don't think/like/want... *that*

It was a constant struggle for me to have my opinions affirmed or acknowledged. Mom went to great lengths to get me to conform or measure up to her standard; for instance, she made me wear girdles in elementary school, reinforcing the fat message.

While typical mother-daughter tension around clothing choices or limits to curfews and activities might explain many of the issues between us, I think there was something else at play.

I now believe my mother's lack of self-esteem shadowed many of her actions. I didn't understand how seriously low it was nor how it connected to perfectionist behaviours.

A lack of apparent support or love from her parents, abusive behaviour by her father toward a niece, and what might have happened in her childhood home, would be cause enough to impact self-esteem and make her protective of a daughter. Research also suggests that low self-esteem can lead to unhealthy perfectionist behaviours, such as unreasonably high expectations for oneself and for others. Perfectionists set the bar high and can make themselves miserable trying to achieve an impossible ideal.

My mother was a perfectionist. She was foremost hard on herself; for instance, she was an excellent seamstress but because her work was not perfect, in her opinion, she gave it up. She was never happy with anything she did. There would always be something that was not right with a meal she cooked, or a family gathering she planned, or a job she did.   Ditto the behaviour and opinions of her daughter.

Perfectionists are concerned about what other people think, and a good number project their perfectionist tendencies toward others around them.

The pressure on an only daughter was tremendous. Even as she tried to make me into her, perhaps even a better "perfectionist" version of herself, the low self-esteem and perfectionism got in the way. Nothing I did measured up. As a perfectionist, her need to direct and control everything around her was like one needs air-it's integral to how a perfectionist operates. Since perfection does not exist, and I would not be controlled, (or so I thought) the result was a lot of unhappiness between us.

I was constantly fighting against every effort I perceived as her control of me and fighting for the confidence that I was maturing into a capable adult. But I was not only fighting Mom, as her ideas were reinforced by society's expectations regarding women.

Girls can't do that.

Be a lady.

Sit still.

The messages were everywhere. My Grade 8 principal told us girls that we were to "stand and be pretty and wait for the boys to ask you to dance" at our graduation party. The Boy Scouts visited the east coast and attended Expo 67 while the Girl Guides stayed home and learned to darn socks. I quit. In high school, my history teacher told me I could not apply for a town job to work on road construction because I was female. I guess only teen boys can read stop signs and direct traffic.

The part of me that fought against this double standard caused me to make some odd decisions, such as not taking typing in high school. I feared it would slot me into becoming a secretary—what I considered a typical female job. I dreamed of something different. The guidance counselor at our high school mocked me.

"Oh, you're the one who wants to do something different," he laughed. I had to search on my own for the post-secondary programs that would get me on the right path.

When I was working as a reporter, out in the world meeting lots of different people, my mother expressed the wish that I worked in a clerical role in a business, so I would "meet a nice businessman to marry."

As I continue to reflect on our relationship, I suspect Mom was as much a victim of societal expectations as I. She was the "Mother," and she took her role seriously, not always balancing the need to be role model versus the need to be a real human to her daughter. And, as her children, we had our expectations as well. I remember coming home once and she wasn't there. Concerned, my brothers and I had gone to the neighbours asking about our mother's whereabouts, but eventually she arrived home. Riding in a convertible, no less, smiling and laughing after a friend had unexpectedly arrived to take her out. She was angry we had raised an alarm with the neighbours; no doubt we had shattered her fun afternoon and embarrassed her.

Ironically, it was my father who encouraged my dream of doing or being something else. When I said that maybe I would consider nursing, he prodded me, "Why not a doctor?" When I thought about being a reporter, he guided me to contact my cousin Joyce, who was doing just that—in fact, had started her own newspaper and had authored a book.

Unfortunately, Mom's words on that summer's day had lasting, albeit unintended, consequences. I was left feeling I still needed to prove to her that I was an adult and could control my own life. I could not have articulated this at the time. Instead, I took this unmet need into my marriage and spent close to 30 years trying to stake my independence within my marriage, with a husband who saw me as capable and didn't understand my insecurities. It made for a tangled web of emotions that only a professional counselor could help me begin to unravel. Mom had this part right: marriage is hard work, and it takes two. Amen to that.

How could Mom, lacking self-confidence and with a low view of her own self-worth, pass those things along to a daughter? If I could, I would tell both my younger self and young Ginger: you are capable, worthy, and thoughtful human beings. Believe in yourselves.

Of course, I am not entirely without some confidence or the internal spunk that forced a playpen around the house. And Dad passed what he could along to me in his own way.

Chapter 39

Building Confidence

Saturday, March 15, 1944
My Darling: ... We fired about five hundred bullets each from a four-gun turret. The four guns fire 80 rounds a second, so it only took five seconds of actual firing to get rid of them. Every fifth bullet was a tracer, and you could see them go through the target, hit the water, and skip away up in the air. The bullets cost ten cents each and when you press the firing button for one second, it costs eight dollars. Besides firing the guns, we set off some star signals, distress signals and the like. They were like huge skyrockets and burnt at about five hundred feet. The firecrackers were worth about twenty-five dollars. All in all, we spent about a thousand dollars' worth of ammunition in no time. No wonder they need to float another victory loan–eh? I guess by this time Larry must have shot away a small fortune... Take care of yourself and Rick and don't work too hard. I love you, I love you, I love you, I love you, I love you, Murray.

Murray and Kim

Toronto, summer, circa 1973

"Brake. Now!"

My father's loud and authoritative voice boomed from the passenger seat, and I reacted, hitting the car brakes hard, coming to an abrupt sudden stop, inches behind the police car.

It was rare for Dad to raise his voice at me. Not unheard of, but rare. In this case, he was allowed because he had done for me what I could never do with my own children—that is to sit calmly in the passenger seat beside an inexperienced driver.

How inexperienced? When we left our small town two hours earlier, I had never driven on the 401 or in big-city Toronto. In fact, as we left Listowel on the two-lane highway, my father had to tell me: "Kim, when a car is coming from the other direction, you don't have to slow down. Keep your speed up."

I walked everywhere, even though the year I turned 16, I had my license within 4-6 weeks, taking classes offered through our high school. In small-town Ontario, a driver's license was gold to any young person. There was no other way to get around. In later years, I heard of some research that suggested 16 is not an ideal age to learn how to drive because of brain development. My hometown had the anecdotal evidence to back that research; it seemed like every other weekend, another youth died in a car accident. The deaths impacted me, and I was a nervous driver. I seldom asked for the car. When I was 20 and planning my second year of school at Ryerson in Toronto, Mom offered me the car to go apartment hunting with my girlfriend. I was shocked by her offer and hadn't even thought of asking for it. I was able to successfully take us to Toronto that time, using explicit directions from Mom. I was also aided, I am sure, by the fact my father had already forced me to drive there once.

I can't recall the reason for our father-daughter trip to Toronto after earning my newly minted license, but Dad was firm. "You are driving."

"Okay," I said, "but I am **not** driving on the 401." The 401 is a multi-lane, high-speed route with multiple exits and other multi-lane highways snaking over and under it as it winds its way across Toronto. I was adamant. I could not drive the 401.

Dad continued his coaching, and I got us out of town and through Kitchener. He taught me how to assure myself that my car was in the middle of my lane: from my position behind the wheel, the hood's centre ornament appeared to line up with the edge of the road. I still miss that feature on the more stream-lined designs.

"Tell me when we get to the 401," I reminded him. Clearly, I had little sense of direction; nor had I paid attention the multiple times I made this same trip with my parents, albeit in the backseat.

I continued to follow my father's directions, turn here, turn there, and then I was steering around a slight curve and as the car straightened out, my father gave his next direction: "Now, hit the gas and don't stop."

As I applied pressure to the gas pedal, I yelled, "Is this the 401? Oh no, I am on the 401."

And there I was, sailing along between 50 and 60 miles per hour while my father read his Time magazine and hummed. Radiating calm.

The only near-miss came at the end when it was time to slow down, and my warped sense of speed had us traveling faster than I realized. I didn't hit the police car, and I had a new sense of what I could accomplish. Even if my knees were shaking. Thanks to my calm father.

If Dad had nerves of steel for driving, then Mom held court in the kitchen, even if her cooking skills took some good-natured ribbing over the years.

Chapter 40

The Dining Room Table

Thursday, August 10, 1944
"Darling Ginger: I'll be seeing you tomorrow night. PS Tell Rickey the three of us will have 'pupper' on the train someday. Love, Murray"

Ginger

When Bill was 9, he entered a writing competition that asked contestants to explain why they have the best mom in the world. Bill wrote: "My Mom makes great Jell-O."

It's a cute tale, but what sealed its place in family lore is that his winning submission earned Bill a small record player. Sixty-plus years later, he still remembered the record player was the second-place prize. First place was a coveted bicycle.

Mom, on the other hand, never lived down the reputation that her cooking skills of making great Jell-O made her a mom to be honoured. Dad repeated this story often.

Some women are naturals in the kitchen. They don't need a recipe and are inventive cooks for their families; they relish preparing and serving meals for any size of crowd and seem to do so at the snap of a finger.

None of that describes Mom.

Canned and prepared food were staples. She didn't bake. She planned her meals and made notes for herself about when to put food on and when to take it out. A major concern for her was getting everything on the table still hot.

My cousin Joyce recalled Mom phoned to tell her that the butcher had left a package of meat with "riles" written on it. Not understanding what "riles" were or how to cook them, she told Joyce, "You're an excellent cook. I'll give these to you." When Joyce opened the package, she discovered the riles were ribs, the "b" looking like an "l" and an "e." Mom insisted Joyce keep them because she would not know how to cook ribs either.

Regardless of her protests that she was not a good cook, we were well-fed children, but it was the basics. Breakfast in the winter before school was always oatmeal with rivers of brown sugar, toast, orange juice, and hot chocolate. Peanut butter and strawberry jam or grilled cheese sandwiches were lunch, with

perhaps a bowl of Campbell's tomato soup. The occasional pizza, made with a store kit, was about as exotic as it got; meat and potatoes were standard fare. French fries were a favourite treat made in Mom's deep fryer.

<Despite the teasing, Mom's meals were delicious, and she was a superb hostess.

One dish Dad loved and nicknamed "poor man's meal" was hamburger and mashed potatoes. Mince and tatties in Scotland. Mom added water to fried hamburger and onion, creating a soup/gravy. She would scoop and pour it over a well of mashed potatoes. Some ketchup and pickles made it great comfort food on cold winter days.

Some of Mom's dishes became family favourites. One of these was a Jell-O dish (her speciality!), made with grape Jell-O and bing cherries. Her curried fruit was a tasty side with ham or turkey. Pork barbecue was popular when there was a large crowd. Family applauded when she lit the rum on the Christmas pudding and served it at the table with a blue ring of fire on top. She served it with cavity-inducing hard sauce, frozen slices of icing sugar and butter.

Despite teasing our mother about her cooking, I suspect one of our family's favourite memories is dinners in the dining room at 485 Wallace Ave. in Listowel. It certainly is mine.

Their two-storey brick home was on one of the major streets that runs through town, with a large front verandah that served as an additional room for family in warmer weather. A white wooden railing ran between stone pillars at the corners. At one end was a swing with an assortment of lawn chairs set around side tables filling the space in front of the living room window. When I was small, they cut the centre pillar of a round wooden table so it would sit lower to the wooden porch floor. A perfect spot to play board games or with my dolls. Or to set snacks for family gatherings.

Inside the front door, just to the right, was a sweeping curved staircase leading up to the second floor. Straight ahead, the entrance hall ended with the mirrored door of a coat closet. To the left was the living room, which featured pocket doors in the walls that divided the living room from the entrance hall. Mom always left these inside their pockets. From the living room, looking toward the back of the house, the dining room was next, framed by two white round pillars.

The dining room was large, taking up the full width of the house with a 10-foot ceiling. The space was impressive. It was the physical centre of the house, but I would argue that it was also the heart of the family home. When the table was fully extended, with a small extension for one end built by my father, all of us could sit together for a meal. There was no child's table. We all sat together. Sometimes that was as many as 20 people, including spouses, dates, and grandchildren. Even with the table extended, you could still walk through the room from the living room to the kitchen on the other side. At the far end of the room were built-in cupboards and sideboards, which displayed glassware and special dishes. There was a narrow, deep closet in the room that ran under the front hall stairs. We dubbed this "Rick's room" in his absence. Mom's table linens, fresh from the dry cleaners, were hung in here.

This room also held mom's sewing machine and the table was the perfect size to layout patterns on material. Mom did some sewing, but her perfectionist tendencies made her unhappy with results, and she was more inclined to ask someone else to sew for her. This room is also where we did homework. I can remember hand-writing essays at the table in high school. When there was lots of company around, it served as the card table where "31" was the popular game, but instead of shouting 31, we had to call "Ram Damn" instead. At the end of a round, Mom would sing, "Put a nickel in the pot, in the nickelodeon" as the losers would place their nickels, or sometimes pennies, into a jar to hold the game cache.

But for family dinners, the room was unmatched. My parents held equal court at each end of the table. Between them, a white linen tablecloth was the canvas on which my mother arranged good dishes, silverware, and as a centrepiece, flowers and candles. Always candles. My mother knew how to set a mood.

Thanksgiving, Listowel, circa 1975

I stand at the kitchen counter watching Dad carve the turkey, his dress shirtsleeves pushed up to his elbows to avoid the grease. He arranges slices of white and dark meat on a large platter. The air is warm and rich with smells of traditional thanksgiving turkey and stuffing. The sound of the beaters promises fluffy whipped potatoes. I'm beside Dad at the double sink, washing pots with hot, soapy water to keep ahead of the dirty dishes.

<Dad carving and mom supervising, circa 1980s

Dad is telling me a story about when he was little, and they didn't get frozen turkey from the grocery store. "I remember Dad came into our kitchen carrying a live bird. He was holding it by its feet, and it was flapping its wings and he placed it right next to where I was sitting, and it terrified me. I was just a little guy. It was the same size as me." He laughs at a memory he cherishes.

"The meat is carved," Dad announces as he not-so-discreetly places a few small morsels of moist turkey into his mouth; "Mm. It's perfect, hon," he assures Mom.

"Where's the wishbone?" I ask, and he points to it on the kitchen windowsill in front of us, where it is drying for pulling and granting wishes later.

Mom is filling serving dishes with hot candied carrots and green beans as Bev and Linda take them from the kitchen and place them on the dining room table. Family is called from the living room, the front porch, and the tv room to come to the table.

We fill the house because everyone is home.

Everyone finds their seats, guided by some unspoken arrangement; everyone knows left-handed Bill gets that end chair on Dad's right and I sit at the other end to Mom's left. Jan is pouring wine into glasses. Miles selects the right music on the Hi-Fi. Dad calls for grace, something he only does in the dining room when the family is home. For an agnostic, he does an amazing job of thanks, not only for the food, but for the family gathered.

Spoons click against serving dishes, there's an occasional call for cranberry sauce, or butter, and Rosemary Clooney croons, "Come on a my house" in the background. Butter melts on croissant rolls, warm and lightly browned from the oven, on matching bread and butter plates. From her end of the table, Mom serves piping hot sweet potatoes, swimming in butter and brown sugar, onto offered plates. Quiet descends as we enjoy the meal–including Jell-O! Mom is glancing at everyone's plates.

"Miles, eat some vegetables." Scott smiles at Grandma, telling his uncle to eat his vegetables.

"Rick, do you have enough? What about you, Linda?"

"We're good, Mom. Everything is delicious."

Dad looks around the table. "I wonder what the poor people are doing tonight?" A reminder that we have more than enough.

Or sometimes in a strong feigned English accent: "Here we suffer grief and shame, across the road they do the same. And a damn sight worse next door." I'm not sure where this comes from.

Bill calls for a toast to the cook, and we take a sip of wine. Dad keeps his wineglass in the air and calls Mom's attention.

"Hey Ging. May the wings of love never lose a feather, 'til my *big boots and your little shoes go under the bed together."*

Mom smiles and raises her wine glass. Sometimes there is a second toast.

"I'm above you, I'm below you, may I always be your equal."

The candlelight gives everyone and everything a warm glow; we are all here. I look around the table, listening to snippets of conversation. The family is growing and changing. My parents are getting older. I wish everything could stay just the way it is right now. I want to hold the moment, if only I could bottle it.

I excuse myself and disappear into the back stairway, dabbing the tears away. They would tease mercilessly if they knew how emotional I felt. Wearing my heart on my sleeve, again.

Perhaps because I was the youngest and last to leave, I would become overjoyed when my older siblings came home, to the point of private tears one time. When Rick and Linda came home with their four children, it brought Bill, Jan, and Miles home as well. Over the years that grew to include Kathy and Bev. As time went by, the occasions when everyone was there became fewer and fewer.

After Dad's funeral, we sat around the table, but no one took Dad's end chair. And the family never gathered in the dining room again.

Mom took a lot of teasing about her Jell-O and her A&P apple pie, a frequent choice for dessert, but I would defy any of my brothers to deny that they would give anything to sit around that dining room table one more time to enjoy not only the company, but the bountiful meal that was served with love.

And we would stay late to enjoy Dad's after-dinner entertainment.

Above, at their 50th anniversary with Marjorie and Pete; > with Rick and Linda who celebrated 25 years the same month.

< Mom and Dad circa early '60s. And below, smiling at home, circa '80s.

Classic Dad, smoke swirling from the pipe, reading, and likely humming. Probably asked me to thump his back after this picture was taken, to help with the asthma. Mom at her last Thanksgiving with Rick, Kim, Jan, Miles. Dad wanted Mom to keep colouring her hair, so Mom kept it dark until Dad died. Then she had a beautiful gray. But she was a shell of her former self in many ways over the four years she lived without him.

Chapter 41

After-Dinner Entertainment

March 14, 1944
... I love you sweetheart. I love you. I really do love you. Remember the night I first kissed you? Remember when I first spoke to you? Remember Long Branch Park on a warm summer evening? Remember how on such nights, I used to meet you, and take you home? Remember our first date, and the day I gave you your ring?... Good night and kisses to you both. Murray.

Murray

I realize now what a gift Dad gave all of us by being so expressive. Taking the time to share his memories, like those in this chapter's letter, clearly served a purpose in building the ties that bind. Reflecting on this vivid connection to my past has strengthened my awareness of the pain and loss experienced by those who have connections to their past severed.

My brothers and I were nurtured by our parents, and Dad's recollections of his own childhood contributed to our family identity.

Listowel Dining Room Circa 1975

Dessert dishes cleared, we call Mom back from the kitchen; Bill collects the liqueur tray off the sideboard and pours small glasses of Amaretto and Bailey's. Jan and Miles are debating some point of memory from childhood. Mom tells them they are nuts, that what they are talking about never happened, and they hoot with laughter.

"That's another escapade Mom never knew about," Jan teases her.

The candles on the table continue to cast a lovely glow as Linda and Bev engage in quiet discussion. Grandchildren play around the table; some are watching television. Dad looks down the long table at Mom and grins.

"That was an amazing meal, Ging. God, I'm full. I shouldn't eat so much."

His eyes might shine with the effects of wine and a full belly, but he is just drunk on the fact family is home.

"Tell us about the time Cassie ran through the factory," someone prompts Dad.

"No. Tell the one about you sleeping out in your tent and that guy running away," says another.

And everyone settles in to listen to Dad's childhood stories.

Dad and his brothers slept in tents in their yard as soon as weather permitted in the spring until the first snowfall in the autumn. It made it easier to get up and into mischief as many of the stories started with "One night we were sleeping in the tent..." The canvas for the tents came from the dump behind the Good Year plant.

"Nothing was holding us back," he recalled.

***

The Dare

"One night, we were sleeping in the tent, but we all got up to see Cassie take a dare. A favourite pastime was to dare someone, and the best guy for taking any dare was Cassie."

Cassie, or Bill Cassman, was a familiar character in Dad's stories. We felt we knew him, although we had never met him.

"The dare this time was to run through an old, abandoned factory down by the tracks - a haunted factory, we believed. We used to shoot cap pistols and play cops and robbers there during the day because the sound of the pistols echoed. But the dare was that Cassie was to run through the factory in the middle of the night.

"So, it's the middle of the night when the gang gets dressed, and we all head to the factory. All of us line up along the embankment by the tracks. We're all excited. It's dark and Cassie is going to run through a haunted factory!

Dad's telling always helped paint a picture. We could see the group of young boys standing in the dark, a little nervous themselves, and excited. Waiting to see a ghost!

"Cassie goes down the embankment to the factory after telling us his plan. 'As soon as I go in, I'll start yelling and if I stop yelling, then you will know I am in trouble.' What we would have done if he stopped yelling, I do not know, but we were to keep an eye out for any ghosts.

"So, Cassie enters the factory at one end, and he's yelling at the top of his lungs 'Ahhhhhh'. And we can trace his progress through the building, our eyes following his voice through to the other end."

At this point in the story, Dad is already laughing at the memory. It's like he is back on that embankment with his friends again. He's almost unable to continue the tale. He wipes one eye with the heel of his hand as he finishes, shaking his head.

*"And out the other end comes not one, but two figures, **both** of them yelling at the tops of their lungs."*

We can see the homeless man, a hobo we would have called him, running to save his life, and Cassie, the kid, running from the ghosts.

"Cassie must have jolted the poor guy out of a sound sleep when he entered the building, yelling at the top of his lungs."

They never knew who was more frightened - the hobo or Cassie - but Dad's memory of the night was so vivid we could see it too.

***

Some of the evening escapades were a bit more dangerous.

Riding the Rails

"One night we were sound asleep in the tent when (Russ) Downey came in to tell us he was going to run away from home. He had a bandana hankie with a razor and a change of clothes hanging on the end of a stick. So, up we get, put on our pants and we go to see Downey off. He was planning to ride the rails."

Riding the rails was a common way for men and women who were looking for work during the depression to get out of paying for a train ticket. They were desperate. They hid along the tracks, and then as the train started, they ran alongside it and attempted to climb aboard. Many lost their lives, or limbs, in the attempt. The railway hired bulls to keep these non-paying people off the train. People who rode the rails would also have to jump off the moving train before it reached a station to avoid the police.

"When we got to the train station, there were about a hundred people at the railway crossing, many planning to ride the rails, I guess. I remember seeing the police approach one young kid, not much bigger than me-around pre-teen-but a large group of people came toward the policeman yelling at him to leave the kid

alone, that he was with them. The policeman, outnumbered, backed off. We said our goodbyes to Downey and went back to our tent to sleep the rest of the night."

Although a dangerous plan, the story had an amusing ending.

"It wasn't too much longer before Downey was back waking us up. What happened? He got on the wrong train! He didn't get on the one that was going out-but on the one that was coming in!"

Dad laughed at the error, but also noted that the police, who sometimes did successfully stop children from this inexpensive, but dangerous mode of transportation, had sent Downey home.

***

It may have been simpler times, but not safer for children. Dad belonged to a gang. The Scarlet Fever Gang. You had to survive this dangerous childhood disease to be a member. "We were a bunch of scraggly, thin, and sickly-looking gang members."

One of the more dangerous stunts they pulled was to walk across the streetcar trestle above Etobicoke Creek. There were no railings-it was not intended for walkers. Sometimes, the streetcar had to stop and wait for them to get off.

"When Mom got word of it, she banned us from going up that way."

Some of their mischief involved behaviours I suspect his mother would have also banned, had she known about them.

***

Nicky Nicky Nine Door
"On Eighteenth Street there was the Booth Brick Yard and a group of apartments. The doors to the apartments were close together, and they opened into the home. We would get rope and

Roberta Kim

tie the door handles of two doors together. Then we would knock on both doors, and as the owners tried to open the doors, we would stand there and laugh. One guy got so livid he came out his back door to chase us. We took off through the asylum grounds.

"Nice kids," Dad added sarcastically, not particularly proud of the behaviour. The asylum was the Lakeshore Psychiatric Hospital on Queen Street in Etobicoke.

"The asylum employed men living in the area. One was a guard who lived down the street, and he would always chase us. So, we always got him to chase us. We would knock on his door and start running toward the lakeshore. Once you got down by the creek, there was a lot of bush. We could go from Fifteenth Street to Sixteenth Street in the trees. We would try to do it without touching the ground. Then we would backtrack and watch him, from high up, run after us. He was good for a chase every night."

***

Another prank that involved running is another one Dad said he wasn't proud of, but it was one we always asked him to tell. The telling of these stories made our father human to us, and I think it was a key to why we wanted his respect more than anything.

***

Scotty
"Scotty was a boarder who stayed at Mrs. Downey's on Fifteenth Street. He worked at the Wine Company, and he would come home loaded every night. He would look at us kids, and he would scare us a bit.

"At the bottom of our street was an old house with a path that

235

cut across the corner, and to the left of the path was a clump of bushes and trees. Old Scotty went in there, I guess, to relieve himself. We knew he was in there. Wondering if he might chase us that night, we started throwing rocks into the bushes.

"Nothing happens. After a while, there is the dare: who will walk down around the path and look into the bushes?"

This time it is Dad who takes the dare, along with his good friend Sam Maxwell and his younger brother Nink.

"We walk, tiptoeing down the path. Pretty soon Scotty came out. We had hit him alright. His head was bleeding, and he came roaring out of there. The chase begins, and I am in the lead."

Dad relives the memory as he tells it.

"I go down toward the village and pass Fourteenth Street. But Nink and Sam turn up Fourteenth Street, and I don't want to be left alone, so I make a U-turn and as I turn down the street, I am only about two steps in front of Scotty. I must have flown. About the time I got up to where the Marshalls lived, I met Mr. and Mrs. Clay. Mr. Clay used to be a guard in the asylum. I tell them: 'Scotty is trying to chase me, and he is drunk.' Mr. Clay put me behind him, and when he reached us, Scotty stumbled and fell. He was a real mess and told them 'The damn kids threw rocks at me.' Mr. Clay convinced Scotty to go the other way, and then he gave me hell for throwing rocks. I was shaking. Just then, Dad came down. Nink had gone home to get him, and Dad had jumped the back fence to come to the rescue."

His father would have been late 50s or early 60s, an age when people are thinking of grandchildren, not rescuing their kids from self-induced trouble. Dad never relayed the specific punishment that followed, but that was the only time the gang threw rocks at Scotty, or anyone.

***

The freedom the children experienced was different from today, and the trouble they caused seems innocent when compared against drugs and gun violence. But consequences were serious enough at times. For instance, the kids from the area had a fort so well constructed, the adults could not find the entry. It was a tunnel, dug down underground. Would-be runaway Russ Downey hid in the tunnel once to get out of school, and the local undertaker, who also served as a truant officer, could not find him. He was close and yelled for Downey, but he never found him. Later, the city cleared the area to reshape a road, and a horse went through the tunnel to the fort, unfortunately ripping its leg on the items stored there.

Dad's tales would remind us of how different his childhood was from ours. There was a blacksmith shop between Sixth and Seventh streets where the boys just stood and watched, never chased away. "We were not too much out of the Huck Finn age when I think of that." Dad positioned this memory against watching the first man on the moon in 1969 marveling at the changes he saw over his lifetime. Revelry Hardware Store sold harnesses and buggy whips and Archibald's Meats delivered to homes using a cutter in the winter. The driver allowed kids to hang on for a ride; "when the horse opened up across a field, we went flying through the snow."

Dad's 'Huckleberry Finn-like' childhood, his stable home, and the couple who nurtured him with love were significant factors in shaping the man that Ginger fell in love with in the mid-1930s. To her, he embodied something solid and secure, something better than she knew.

Chapter 42

The Laws of Attraction

March 14, 1944
My dear Ginger...You called me down for not writing to you...I was
really worried about you and Rick myself. You must remember this is
about the fourth or fifth letter from me and to-day is the first I have
heard from you...I was so glad to hear from you and yet I write a letter
like this. I can't make it out ...Write again soon Sweetheart. Good
night and kisses to you both. Murray"

Murray and Ginger

It's a universal truth, I suspect, that children do not think
about their parents as young lovers, capable of jealousies, fears,
or hurt hearts. As I matured, I came to understand Murray and
Ginger had a life as a couple, separate from being my parents. I
speculated about their relationship, and I sometimes wondered
if Dad loved Mom, more than Mom loved Dad. I might be
forgiven that perception, as Dad was the more demonstrative of
the two. Comfortable in his own skin, raised in a home with
love, he had no qualms about showing how much he loved her.

Listowel, circa 1967, a Saturday morning
I am chewing a piece of toast, softened by a generous spread

of butter, and I enjoy the sweet warmth and scratchy sensation as the toast slides down my throat. Brenda Starr, Reporter, dazzles with her big red hair and eyes like stars from the pages of the colour comics. Across the kitchen table, Mom pours herself another cup of Bokar coffee and stirs in the thick Carnation milk and two teaspoons of sugar. She lights another cigarette. We hear Dad coming down the front stairs, two very large rooms away from the kitchen where the aroma of Mom's coffee and the sound of toast popping announce morning. Dad's humming, a habit developed because of his asthma, sounds a declaration throughout the house: Dad is up! There is no tune or rhythm, just a loud humming that goes up or down or through slight variations. "Hmmmm, ahhhh, nnnn, hmmmmm." He arrives in the kitchen with the scent of soap and Listerine in the air, his morning ablutions completed.

"Good morning honey," he smiles at me. I'm not old enough yet to develop the morning attitude that will come in the next few years, so I smile in greeting.

He addresses my mother: "Good morning, sweetheart. God, you're beautiful in the morning. I am going to kiss you. I am going to kiss you on the neck."

I sit back to watch the show, one I have seen before but never tire of watching. Mom glances over at me with an amused expression on her face. My father stands behind her chair as he announces the play-by-play. "Right here, on the back of your neck. I will lift your hair off the nape of your neck. It's a beautiful neck. See, I am lifting the hair. Now, I will bend and give you a loud..." And a very loud, exaggerated kissing sound accompanies the action of his bending over to place his lips on the back of her neck.

"Oh, Murray, stop that," my mother admonishes. And I wonder

why she does that. Doesn't she love him the same?

No one can really know what goes on between a married couple. That's one pearl of wisdom my mother pronounced about marriage. As the only one of five children in her family to remain in one marriage, her observation that marriage is hard work had credibility. Even one of Dad's brothers was divorced.

"Why do you and Dad stay married?" I asked her, curious, and maybe looking for reassurance.

"Sometimes people just give up," she responded. Rather than staying through the rough times.

When we heard of couples divorcing, she expressed frustration when gossipers tried to assign blame. "It takes two people to make a marriage, and it takes two to end a marriage," she asserted.

<Over the years, from the top, while dating, their 40th wedding anniversary, and at Dad's retirement party.

"Marriage is hard work, and it's even harder after you have children." She was emphatic on one point: if you don't have a strong marriage, having children will tear it apart, not strengthen it.

No doubt, having five children created its own strain on their marriage. They had nine months after their wedding to settle into their life before being disrupted by the first-born. Then a war. Then the remaining four of us arrived within two to four years of each other-one just out of diapers and the next one into them. Like others of her generation (and past generations), my mother spent much of her time between the ages of 22 and 40 either pregnant or running after toddlers, while her husband pursued his career. It was an arrangement that worked for them, but no doubt took a toll.

While the family divorce rate fuelled my many questions about marriage, it may also have been the reason I got upset when they fought.

Fighting is an inevitable result of two people living together, she tried to assure me. One place where tensions often rose was in the car. I hated it so much that I hung my ankles over the back of the front seat bench and waved my feet between them. They stopped while Mom assured me that all couples fight, that you can't expect two people to live together without having differences. Quiet would reign for a few minutes, and then one would start back up and eventually the bickering was on again. There were never physical fights, just words, and they didn't last very long. The words were not personal, but each could be stubborn in their own way. There would be an outburst, and then they would be back to normal. I can't even remember what the fights were about. Sometimes it was about directions, or Dad's inattention at the wheel. "Hey kids, look at that!"

While my parents had a very traditional marriage, Mom didn't play the role of meek and mild wife giving into her man's every whim. That truth became amusingly clear in a document a friend passed to Miles after Dad's death. The document is a copy of an elementary school report written by Robert Dodkin in 1975 when he was about 11. His teacher assigned homework to interview someone about the depression, and Robert chose Dad. The handwritten report followed a simple format of "Interviewer" followed by the question and then "Dadson" followed by Dad's response. At the bottom of page two is the following exchange:

Interviewer: Did you support Roosevelt and Bennett?

Dadson: "I didn't care too much, but I liked them."

Dadson's wife: "I didn't like Bennett."

Robert had carefully noted both responses to this one question. His report earned him a healthy 93 per cent. Maybe the teacher gave a bonus mark for handling two opinions with diplomacy.

Listowel, February 14, circa 1972

It's Valentine's Day and as I walk through the dining room, I notice a basket on the table. In the basket, there's a bottle of wine, a loaf of Italian bread, and a note in Dad's handwriting. "A loaf of bread, a bottle of wine, and thou, is all I need." (1)

I walk into the kitchen and Mom is there. That's a romantic gift from Dad, I say. She seems to dismiss it with a wave of her hand.

< Mom and Dad at Rick and Linda's wedding, 1965. Only Ginger could rock such a hat!

What about love, I pried. The thing of movies, she replied. And yet, when she spoke of their years of courtship when they were young, it sounded like pure romance. Perhaps she wanted to balance the romantic impression those stories left, so I would better understand it wasn't all roses.

She told me once that she put Dad on a pedestal. That's not a suitable spot for anyone to live, but she had a difficult time expressing love; her devotion to her family was the action that expressed her feelings.

There are many theories about why people are attracted to each other. According to author Harville Hendrix PH.D., couples unconsciously fulfil each other's unmet childhood needs.

That's easy to identify with my mother. Alcoholic parents, the shadow or reality of abuse, and being banished by extended family resulted in no self-esteem. Murray showered her in it. His love for her gave her the self-confidence to be the best version of herself. My father's unmet childhood need is a bit more difficult to determine, as he appeared to have an idyllic childhood. His constant caring for and providing for Ginger was perhaps a way for him to channel a buried desire to take care of his beloved mother, whose death hit him hard. One of his biggest stated fears was poverty in his old age, that he would end up in a "6 by 9-foot room," reliant on his children-as happened to his father. Out of this fear, he refused to sell the big old house in Listowel, despite pleas from my mother. He believed, as it turned out correctly, that the house would be her old age security after he died.

The sale of the house supported her when Dad's pension stopped on his death. In this last act of devotion, he continued to care for her, even after death.

(1) *Paraphrase of Omar Khayyam, famous classical Persian poet who wrote: "A loaf of bread, a jug of wine and thou is all I need."*

Chapter 43

Who's First?

Thursday, March 23, 1944
P.S. I guess you think I'm nuts, but I do miss you Ging and never -
never could I love anyone but you.

Murray and Miles, Ginger and Kim

A conversation between son and father:

"At the end, it has to be your mother first. If I died first, she could not look after herself. She's just a girl."

Another conversation between daughter and mother:

"At the end, it has to be your father first. If I died first, he would not be able to go on."

No time stamp on the conversations, but both took place years before anyone became ill or faced death. It was only 25 plus years after they were both gone that my brother and I shared the conversations with each other.

Is it a sign of true love when you would rather bear the pain of someone's death than have them live that kind of hell?

Chapter 44

Till Death, or Longer

"All day tomorrow, I'll be loving you and then, on the day after forever, I'll start right in again." - Lyrics written and sung by Frank Sinatra

Murray and Ginger

Perhaps it is fitting that it was Sinatra's song that was an earworm in my mind when Mom died four years after Dad. The famous entertainer also died in 1998, although it wasn't his voice that I remembered. Dad often sang these words to Mom, ending in a low, sultry tone on the word 'again'.

By legal definition, my parents' marriage ended shortly after their 54th wedding anniversary. My father held on until the early hours of July 1, when he finally, and mercifully, let go. He was angry to leave; he didn't make plans the way Mom did four years later when she faced a terminal diagnosis. As though she was preparing to join him, she dry-cleaned her "going away dress," borrowing the term women traditionally used for the outfit they would don after stepping out of their wedding dresses, for her cremation. Her rose-coloured dress would complement the grey casket she also requested.

One of Dad's favourite poems was given to him by Bill, and it hung in our kitchen for years. Desiderata became a mantra for Dad: "No doubt the universe is unfolding as it should." I think it gave him some comfort as he had years earlier turned his back on a belief there was anything to follow his death. He would get angry with me if I ever talked about him not dying or staying young forever.

"You will see me in my casket, and that's the way it should be," he would tell me. Sometimes calmly, sometimes more forcefully. Mom said he took his own mother's death very hard, and I have considered that he wanted to better prepare me for what was coming.

He said he didn't want a funeral service; "flush me down the toilet and sing 'Tight as a Drum.' (And I did sing it under my breath as a minister, who had the thankless task of speaking at the funeral of a man he had never met, visibly winced when he repeated another of the lines from Desiderata, "Be at peace with God, whatever you perceive him to be.")

< Dad on the side porch in Listowel before they closed it in.

My Dad was my hero. Have a question? Ask Dad. Want to discuss an issue? Ask Dad. Want to understand something? Ask Dad. Want to know the right thing to do? Ask Dad. When I was younger, I used to caddy for him on the golf course just to spend time with him. He had four sons, but it was his daughter who went into the attic with him to help with insulation. He told me I was pretty, and he believed I was smart. He would sing to me, "We belong to a mutual, admiration society, me and my gal."

I knew when I was younger that my parents were older than some of my friends' parents, and I always worried about losing them. So, when Dad had a stroke in the late 1980s, I was not prepared for him to be ill. Nor was he. However, he could not ignore the arrhythmia in his heart a few years later; the hospital used a fibrillator to get his heartbeat into a regular rhythm.

"I'm not ready to die. There's still more to learn," he told me from his hospital bed.

Eventually, a diagnosis of multiple myeloma was made and then came what would be the final hospital stay, although he desperately wanted to come home. Mom was terrified of him dying at home. They kept him on powerful drugs for the pain and an allergy to morphine caused some strange behaviour. Dad could be tolerant when dealing with people, but there was a side to him where he did not suffer fools gladly, and he could be very impatient. Pain did nothing to mitigate this tendency.

He received blood transfusions after which he would regain energy, so much so that one day I arrived to find him striding down the hall toward me, but my joy at seeing him up soon turned to confusion as he forcefully pushed right into me and was backing me up toward the exit while yelling, "Get out. Get out." Nurses suddenly appeared and they expertly and carefully turned him around. He looked at me like I had betrayed him. So strong was his desire to get out of the hospital, he saw me as an escape plan.

I resolved to bring him home, if only for a short period. My daughter and I arrived one day and announced we would take him home for lunch. I got him to the van and into the passenger front seat. I did not know how to collapse the wheelchair, so I put the van's rear seat down and somehow picked the chair up and forced it into the back.

We drove home, like co-conspirators, and I left him sitting in the wheelchair at the back door as I went in to surprise Mom and to cajole her into putting on a cheerful face. She was afraid he would refuse to go back, and I must admit, I had the same concern. I would not put it past him to grab the steering wheel to divert returning to the hospital. I brought his wheelchair around to the front porch and helped him up the stairs. Hugs were given and received; despite the weakness of the effort, they came with Dad's customary sound effect of "e..e..e" with each squeeze. Mom brought out a sandwich with iced tea, and Dad enjoyed his last lunch on the front porch at 485 Wallace.

On another day, as I pushed his chair around the courtyard at the hospital, Dad broke down and cried, "She doesn't love me." My heart broke for them both. Mom drove from Listowel to Palmerston every day to sit with him, and she was battling her own fears in the vast house by herself. She moved her bed from their bedroom into the dining room on the main floor.

On their last anniversary, the cafeteria sent a special tray of food to the room, but only Mom was eating. He died two days later, and we all watched our once independent, lively, and opinionated mother shrink from life. She refused any offers of help, answering the door in her housecoat when a family friend and Hospice volunteer came, pre-arranged, to take her to a group session dealing with grief. At our nephew's wedding the following year, she stayed in her hotel room while everyone else partied around the pool; if Dad had been there, she would have been out circulating in the crowd, laughing, and enjoying the party. At breakfast the following morning, she tried, awkwardly, to pay my brother back for a coffee.

I had an epiphany: Ginger didn't know how to "be" without Murray.

A lack of nutrition caused her skin to age. She thrived on coffee and cinnamon swirls for breakfast; dinner was minimal. She also enjoyed her wine, so when she called me one evening and her words sounded a bit slurred, I thought she had just removed her teeth and had enjoyed a couple glasses of wine. I never dreamed arterial lateral sclerosis was robbing her of speech, nor that the wine she drank was going directly into her lungs.

As soon as the therapist traced the fluid with a stethoscope, she immediately ordered my mother to stop eating or drinking anything, and a battery of tests in London eventually discovered the cause. While waiting for the results, she agreed to a feeding tube. In the last six months of her life, her skin tone and complexion returned to a healthier appearance. It was disturbing to see her physically look better, while living in fear the disease could cause her to choke to death on her own saliva.

Her preparations to rejoin Murray began.

Chapter 45

Who's Calling?

Thursday, August 10, 1944
Darling Ginger: I am glad to hear that you and Rickey have had a day
out at the Port. Henry and Helen are the best of friends, and I just
know you must have had an enjoyable time.

Ginger, Jan, and Kim

Listowel 1998

"Kim!"

The disembodied voice calling my name from somewhere above startled me. I dropped the intravenous cord. My eyes locked with Jan's across the hospital bed.

It's amazing how many thoughts can cross your mind in nano seconds.

We were on either side of mom's hospital bed, and I had been showing my brother how we could send her more morphine if she needed it. She lay peacefully sleeping between us. The small mechanism fit in the cradle of my hand, and my thumb hovered over the end where the button was located. We could just press the button to administer more drug. Our eyes had connected, and I knew the same thought had occurred to both of us.

She was semi-comatose, ALS taking over more of her internal organs, slowing shutting down operations.

Would she want us to speed-up the process?

Could we even?

Then I heard a voice call my name, and it felt like my sombre thoughts were exposed.

Who had called my name? Was it...?

Then I realized the voice was still speaking, coming over the intercom above her bed.

"Your brother Rick is on the phone. Do you want to speak to him?" the nurse asked.

I ran from the room to take the call.

Chapter 46

Keep Your Sticks on the Ice

Tuesday, Mar. 14, 1944
My Dear Ginger: ... Remember the night I first kissed you? Remember
when I first spoke to you? Remember Long Branch Park on a warm
summer evening? Remember how on such nights, I used to meet you,
and take you home? Remember our first date, and the day I gave you
your ring? Remember our wedding day and the following two weeks?
... Love Murray

Rick, Bill, Jan, Miles, and Kim

Listowel, Fall 1998

"Keep your sticks on the ice."

Mom's message took me back by surprise. It was scrawled on
the whiteboard, her method of communicating since ALS
robbed her of coherent speech.

It wasn't that she was giving motherly advice concerning our
behaviour after her death that surprised me; it was the sports
idiom. I had never heard my mother use hockey lingo, but I
guess years of Dad watching the game must have rubbed off on
her.

After her death, my four brothers and I gathered in her living room to discuss what we should do with her possessions, keeping the hockey stick message in mind.

Despite the sadness, the task was also sweet as we bantered back and forth. The conversation was peppered more with "you should" rather than "I want" such as "Jan, you should take the little stool." He had made it for Mom years ago as a school or scouting project. My parents always boasted about how strong it was. He took it back with pride.

We were doing a pretty good job of keeping our sticks on the ice and in play. Then it came to the silverware.

"Bill, you should take that," I said. "You always admired it." But Bill shook his head.

"I never entertain anymore. It would be wasted on me. Kim, you should take it."

Jan jumped in: "Yes, do that. And then you can have us all to dinner and use the silverware, and we can all enjoy it."

Miles looked at them, aghast. "Wait a minute, guys. Are you sure... you've never tasted Kim's cooking, have you?

So much for sticks on the ice!

Chapter 47

50th Wedding Anniversary

Thursday Mar. 23
P.S. I love you Hon. How about a buck-tooth-kiss?

June 1990
Two Flies

Two flies flew into a grocery store.
They pooped, and they peed all over the floor.
They pooped on the bacon, and they pooped on the ham,
They didn't give a damn for the grocery man.
Chorus
'Cause one was black, and the other was blue,
One had spots on his tra-la-loo.
The other had spots on his tra-la-too,
High ho the derry'o.

Two flies flew up to a map on the wall.
They pooped, and they peed all over it all.
And when those two flies flew away,
You couldn't tell Maine from Ida way....
Chorus

Murray and Ginger

My parents enjoyed good health to celebrate their 50th wedding anniversary in 1990. It was also Rick and Linda's 25th in the same month, so a party of great magnitude was planned. Guests came from both Canada and the United States, included all five children, eight grandchildren, one great-grandson still nestled in his mother's womb, and a host of in-laws, out-laws, and friends.

A hall was rented, a dinner served, and much reminiscing followed.

The day after the party, we gathered around the pool at Miles and Bev's home on Walton Avenue in Listowel. It was cool for the end of June, although the tougher Canadians among us pretended it was quite warm for the benefit of our American family.

Someone, possibly Dad, or Dad egged on by one of us, began to sing "Two Flies."

Now, you must be a Dadson, descended from a Dadson, or related to a Dadson to understand how the singing of this song at this moment was truly one of those magical moments. One in a lifetime of them. Soon, every voice, children AND grandchildren joined in: the point is they ALL knew the words.

At the end of the song, without missing a beat, my mother said, as she often did whenever he broke into one of his army songs, "Oh, Murray. Not in front of the children."

Oh, Mom! And Dad! You played your story out right in front of the children, and the grandchildren, where it deserved to be. Well done.

Your wings of love never lost their feathers, and we hope, if there's a heaven, your shoes are under the bed together!

Acknowledgements

This has been a multi-year project and along the way, I have been supported by several people I want to acknowledge here.

First - my love and thanks to my four brothers, Rick, Bill, Jan, and Miles, who contributed their memories about our parents. In particular, I want to thank Bill, who also provided excellent feedback in the editing process. I am so thankful to have his book cover design: his confidence that I would really do this one day was incredible. I will forever regret I didn't complete this in time for him or Rick to see it. Thank you to Miles and Bev for generously allowing me to use your cottage for a week of solitude and quiet focus at one stage in the process. Thank you both also for helping with the fun tour of Ruthven and the exploration of cemeteries in Windsor and surrounding areas. We got to stay in that delightful inn in Kingsville and revisit some childhood memories in Chatham. I am also grateful that Miles loaned me the CD on which Dad recorded memories of his depression-era childhood. It helped enormously with story details. And it was delightful to hear Dad's voice again.

I wrote the first draft of chapter one of this book in 1999 and dabbled here and there over the years, working on other ideas. But it wasn't until I retired and COVID hit in 2020 that I applied the seat of my pants to the seat of the chair and got serious. I enrolled in GAB (Guided Autobiography) workshops, and I owe thanks to the instructors and other writers I met there. Leigh Morrow and Lily Bengfort, My Story Guides, helped give structure to my scattered thoughts. Fellow student feedback encouraged me to keep doing this for future generations. Thanks also to the members of the online writer's group that provided their feedback and amazing encouragement as well: Sanaz Busink, Seikyee, Melinda Kinghorn, and Janet Hancock.

Research into the Dadson family lineage conducted by my cousin Joyce Beaton-Bihari was phenomenally helpful. While I could add clarity and fill in some of the missing details with the help of ancestry.ca, it is Joyce's meticulously documented research, her own writings, and memories that provided a foundation and helped bring some long-past people to life. Thank you, Joyce, for being an inspiration to me and encouraging me throughout the years.

I pay respect and thanks to my cousin Sharon O'Donovan, who agreed to the telling of her own painful history. It is an important piece of the story to my understanding of Mom, and I am grateful to you, Sharon, for having the courage to tell it and share it.

I thank my lifelong friend Janet Hancock. Who knew that our childhood passion for Nancy Drew books before we parted ways to live different lives in different parts of Canada would lead us to finding a common joy in writing this many years later? (Thanks, Zoom!) Thank you, Janet, for your superb feedback and for lighting that fire we writers need to keep focused on the task. And helping me to bring closure to this project. I look forward to continuing our "writing buddy" talks and to attending more writing retreats with you.

I had the support of my colleague and friend Carolyn McLeod as I neared the end of the project and uploading files to Amazon. Thank you, Carolyn, your design skills were invaluable in preparing the cover and for enhancing many of the old photographs. Thanks for the laughs when we meet and keeping our connection alive.

Of course, the person who has listened to me talking about this Fred and that Fred and this George and that George, or this Jessie and that Jessie and Mae and Lydia, and Margaret Stewart ... possibly ad nauseam ... and who also toured the cemeteries with me, is my husband Jim. Before we married, I told him-writing is important to me, and I have to do it. Line in the sand. God love him, he thinks I'm a talented writer and doesn't understand why I need to spend so much time editing. Thank you for your confidence in me and for your unshakeable love beneath my wings.

Finally, there's Murray and Ginger. They both, knowingly or perhaps unknowingly, shared the stories that inspired this project. I love you both forever and thank you for the legacy you left each of us.

Author's Notes

Dear Readers:

Time forces us to face all kinds of reality. When I stood with the plastic case of Dad's letters to Mom in 1998, the words she said to me when I was 10 echoed in my mind: "When I die you can read them." I knew I had to do more than just read them. The notion of sharing the letters with family took hold quickly. The case in my hand was evidence of Mom's permission.

I learned a lot through this process. Not just the practical challenges of completing a task of this size, but I still had some living to experience before I could get some things I wanted to say down on paper. Some took time and rewriting and lots of reflection to reach. Bringing closure to the project was made difficult by the realization I was having to say goodbye to my parents again. Cue: tears.

The letters helped to bring the story of "Murray and Ginger" to life, to celebrate our parents, and to provide a record for future generations. The letters also provided a brief insight into training manoeuvres during war; they are a piece of Canadian history.

A marriage is more than two people; it is the joining of two families, and couples bring the dynamics of their childhood relationships into the union. Thus, I wanted to include, as much as possible, their childhood memories, as well as details about their parents and grandparents - the people who influenced their lives. We build a sense of self on the stories of past generations, so I wanted to explore, as much as possible, the ancestral stories. Generational memory exists and knowing more about our ancestors can give us a sense of our connectedness over years.

Dad's voice is memorable through the letters and the stories he left.

But I knew very little about my mother's Ruthven history. She offered nothing in personal recollections, and I wanted to give her a voice. The research uncovered stories of sorrow and joy, medical insights, and it also left a few unanswered questions, some of these far more serious than others. It also opened the door to a sense of pride because of some unknown tales. In short, the history revealed both highs and lows of human behaviour and provided the needed context for the story of two poor kids from New Toronto who became our parents.

In the interest of storytelling and attempting to keep the threads of the story alive (and my readers awake) some historical details were removed, and I include them here.

Great-great-grandfather George Dadson

In Finding Father's Family, one of a series of Grandma Books by Joyce Beaton-Bihari, she shared journal writings from great-great George Dadson (the one who did not die of suicide), and a sample of entries is included here. He has provided an accounting of his work beginning in 1822, when he was just 31 years of age. He may have still been working in his bakery at this time. He wrote:

"In the year 1822, I was one of the Petty Constables of the

Parish and in 1829 I was appointed High Constable of the Hundred by the Magistrates. I had control of all and the management of the Constable work and head over all the inferior offices which were 8 in number for our parish. In December the same year we had many labourers out of work as well as mechanics. They got up a rebellion and mobs of them assembled together and broke machines, very determined to break all they came nigh, and lots assembled together to excite and intimidate the gentlemen and farmers. The consequence was many were brought up to justice, sent for trial and many were transported. I had then heavy work to do night and day and the Magistrates ordered the regiment of Scots Greys and they were all the winter to assist in keeping the peace and were obliged to turn out sometimes in the night to go to the neighbouring parishes where there were riots going on."

Further on, it continues: "I held those said offices 45 years and then gave it up in 1867. I had charge of all the prisoners after the superintendent was appointed and was the Master of the new Lock-up House until the second and large one was built when the officers of Police came there to reside. I was appointed Assistant Overseer and Collector of poor rates in 1840 and am now in the year 1867. I have filled nearly all of the offices of the Parish.

"Oh, I forgot. I was Superintendent of Peace for 4 months in consequence of Mr. Big, the Superintendent, leaving in a great hurry without giving notice to do so. I found many pleasing and teasing things in those offices, too numerous to mention and must give it up for the present. I filled the Office of Surveyor for this Parish 27 years, made great improvements as our roads were very bad and soft, and I made them nearly all hard. The paths in the town too were almost impossible and I commenced *paving them with good York stone, a certain amount every year, till I am pleased to say, all are finished, and every living witness will tell you it improved our town much as well as the property in the town being of more value.*

"I am now a member of the Highway Board as Waywarden for this Parish and have been so from the commencement of the new Highway Act. How much longer I shall be spared to fulfill this office I must leave to the over-ruling power, who knows all things and has been my protector through life and has spared me to see and reach the age of 76 and blessed be His Holy Name, Amen."

In 1876 he wrote:

"Blessed be the name of the Lord for His mercies endureth forever. In His goodness He has pleased to spare me one more year, and thanks be to our Heavenly Father, in tolerable good health, and still doing my duties as assistant overseer and collector of poor rates at the advanced age of 85 years." George Dadson

There are several entries like this and in each one, George thanks God to be "spared" another year!

While on a visit to England to explore family roots, Joyce encountered a librarian who told her that searching was a waste of time, as only important people had their obituaries printed in those days. Call it Dadson determination (stubbornness?), but Joyce persevered and found an obituary for our great-great-grandfather, George. His picture hangs in the Cranbrook Museum.

We already had in our possession a lengthy eulogy, authored by W. J. Chapman, about great-great-grandfather George. My brother Rick brought this back from his visit to England. I share a portion of it here for future generations.

*"In remembrance of Mr. George Dadson, Formally High
Constable, and upwards of 40 years Assistant Overseer, Surveyor
of Highways, and Way Warden, deceased 1st June 1880, in his
90th year, living all his long life in the Town of Cranbrook,
beloved and respected by all, buried in St. Dunstan's Churchyard,
7th June 1880, escorted by a numerous concourse of friends."*
(Sic)

Fred kept a constable's truncheon that belonged to his
grandfather, and it came into my father's possession. It was
displayed in the china cabinet in my childhood home. It was a
solid piece of wood about 10 inches long, covered by a gold-
plated metal with a crown on the end. No doubt it would do
some serious damage if brought down on someone's head.

The eulogy, which is 52 stanzas long, references George's
many pursuits:

> *"High Constable hight, ah! Then was he*
> *With Deputies to boot*
> *And kinching rogues would from them flee*
> *And oft'times leave their loot*
> *"As Road Surveyor, he held the reins,*
> *For years, aye many told;*
> *As Waywarden used his brains,*
> *As time around him roll'd*
> *"As an Overseer, dispensing good,*
> *Assistant 'tis I mean,*
> *For the parish worked, minus hood,*
> *The same as for the Queen*
> *"" Dadson" I knew from my boy-days.*
> *When first I gan to lisp*
> *I loved his manners and his ways*
> *Tho sometimes rather crisp*

Like the bread he used to bake,
The crispness rather good;
Some observations he would make,
And laughter pour's a flood."

Race

I share in the book the oft-repeated memory of Dad's about Jan's comments regarding the Black men as the family packed to leave the U.S. There was more I wanted to say about our family's relationship with race and decided the Author's Notes was the place to share it for future generations.

It was a challenge deciding whether comments on the topic of race and diversity should be included in this memoir. We were-are-a White family that continues to live in predominately White, Anglo-Saxon communities. Our roots are embedded in settler stories, as the story of Margaret Stewart highlights. Race was not a family topic we explored.

We didn't have to because we are White.

A Martin Luther King Jr. quote also summed up my trepidation of approaching this topic here: "Shallow understanding from people of good will is more frustrating than absolute misunderstanding from people of ill will."

As I spent much of 2020-21-22 writing and then editing this memoir, I decided I could not ignore the reckoning that our so-called "polite" Canadian society was facing. On almost a daily basis it seemed.

A global pandemic shut down much of our world in March of 2020. Schools closed, businesses that could pivoted their employees to work from home, others closed (some eventually forever), and we were told to stay home except for essential trips. Wearing a mask over mouth and nose along with frequent hand sanitizing became a habit. Then, just three months into this frightening new world, the death of a 46-year-old Minneapolis resident, George Floyd, on May 25 ignited a spark around the world.

His death was not, shamefully, the only death of a Black man that has sparked justifiable outrage over the years, but as the world halted much of its frenzied activity because of a global pandemic, his murder by a police officer sparked a fire that would not die down. Mr. Floyd's image was captured by street artists on the walls of buildings and public structures not only across the United States, but in Canada and in several European countries. Make-shift memorials sprung up in their wake. Mr. Floyd's gasped "I can't breathe," captured in a bystander's video camera while a White police officer kept his knee on his neck for nine minutes, 29 seconds, became a battle cry of 'Black Lives Matter' protests - also held everywhere. They found the officer who kept his knee in place for all those minutes guilty of murder in a trial held a year later - but it says a lot about our society that we held our breath waiting on the jury's decision. Despite the overwhelming evidence, including a video, it was not a foregone conclusion.

'White privilege' was another phrase that gained in traction and understanding. Those of us born with White skin, regardless of our socio-economic backgrounds, start life with an advantage. While that truth was, and is, difficult for some to accept, our reality is that when people see us, they don't automatically assume we are criminal or dangerous. White Moms don't have to tell our sons to be aware of their actions because people - including the police - will automatically assume these things, based solely on the colour of their skin. I read a post written by a Black father who said he never goes for a walk by himself in the neighbourhood where he lives but takes his young daughter with him. This is because when people see him with her, they see a father, but when he is alone, they see only a Black man and fear is clear in their eyes and actions. Some cross the street. That kind of systemic attitude and belief are difficult to erase just because we may intellectually say they are wrong. It is an attitude that is fed by years of one-sided media images that don't balance the picture.

Then, in March 2021, a man walked into three different spas in Atlanta, Georgia, and gunned down six Asian women, sparking similar discussion and reckoning around the growing hate crimes perpetrated against people of Asian descent. Some of this was rooted in the perception that the COVID-19 virus spreading around the world was China's fault, a belief given credence by a U.S. President who insisted on calling it the Chinese virus. People who lack the education or intellect to research and read credible sources fell prey to the misinformation that abounded on social media.

As Canadians, we may have been feeling smug that these actions were in the U.S., even though they prompted lots of stories of both Black and Asian racism within our own borders. But then June happened, and the world was informed of our shame. The buried bodies of over 200 Indigenous children were discovered at a former residential school in British Columbia. Starting from the early 1900s until the 1990s, Indigenous children were stolen from their parents and placed in residential schools set-up by the government with a policy of taking the Indian out of the child. These children suffered abuse, in all its forms, at the hands of representatives of the religious organizations that ran the schools. Many children died, and it is expected there will be many more skeletons of young children found across the country at other school sites. If they didn't die, they were released back into society at age 18 with no understanding of how to cope on their own, how to parent or how to be a family. They were robbed of their heritage and language. The repercussions continue down multiple generations. Having been able to conduct the research I have on my own family, I can't imagine the grief and frustrations felt by those who had **both** their past **and** their future stolen.

As we were still reeling from the news about the buried children, we learned about the horrendous action of a 20-year-old man in London, Ontario. He drove his vehicle into a Muslim family that was out for a stroll in their neighbourhood on a Sunday evening. Three generations of one family gone at once, leaving a young boy without parents, sister, or grandmother, because of the deliberate actions of one person filled with an inexplicable hate.

My own educational journey concerning race and culture received a boost when I became a teacher at a local college where international students began to change the complexion of our students and the cultural expectations in our classrooms. If a school is a microcosm of society, what I witnessed was a gradual increase from two or three international students in 2010 to classrooms where the majority of students hailed from somewhere other than North America by 2019. I would tell students, aiming to enhance the awareness of White Canadians in the mix, to look around the class and recognize that the diversity they see would be what they would experience in their future work. And I would encourage them to take advantage of this time to get to know each other on a personal level, believing that once we know others, our fears and misconceptions can be alleviated. Some years were better than others as far as achieving some level of success in this goal. As faculty, we had our own work to address, and I credit the college with offering many workshops on understanding the differences in cultures and, importantly, to recognize our own bias. I was (am) not perfect, but my awareness level was raised beyond what it might have been otherwise, and I am grateful for those years.

If nothing else, the years of the COVID-19 pandemic that hit during my last semester before retirement raised collective awareness levels concerning various forms of racism to new heights. I could not ignore the fact my parents lived in Haddonfield, New Jersey, in the 1950s, an era when the impact of a world war was still reverberating along racial lines.

The war had created an opportunity for Black Americans who migrated in great numbers from the south to fill labour shortages. New Jersey's Black population increased by 40 per cent during and after the war between 1940 and 1950. As a war was being fought against racist and anti-democratic actions abroad, it emboldened Black Americans to take action for their own justice. Camden, where the Campbell Soup head plant was located, was one of the larger centres to attract both men and women to jobs that paid better than many had received during the depression. And it appeared the state was progressive, passing in 1945 a Fair Employment Practices Act that forbade discrimination in employment. A Division Against Discrimination was established in the Department of Education. In 1954, when my parents were living there, discrimination was to end in public housing. Time has only proved that, while policy is important, we need implementation by people who believe in it for genuine change. When the war ended, a combination of factors changed the picture. White Americans began to leave for the suburbs, supported by federal highway and housing policies;

the jobs which Black Americans had travelled to fill were drying up as technology in the form of automation replaced them. Ghettos developed as the economy changed.

When people would try to favourably compare Canada's race record with what took place in the U.S., my mother would just state that people needed to live there before commenting, noting that Canadians did not live or work in the racially charged communities of many U.S. cities. Her words came back to haunt me after hearing about the young man who purposely targeted the family of Muslim faith in London, and whenever I become aware of instances of hate motivated by differences in race, culture or religion occurring more frequently in our country as we become increasingly diverse.

The small town where I grew up had one Black family and one Chinese family. Years later, when I told a Black student about my hometown, her reaction was, "wow, they must have been so lonely." It was not a perspective I had thought of, and her comment shone a light on my lack of awareness. I am sure it likely did reflect exactly how both families felt. They were at least lonely. How much racism they experienced, I don't know, but I am not so naïve as to believe it was none.

I saw my parents treat people with respect, but I also heard comments that I now recognize as forms of systemic racism. The words we choose, the jokes we tell, the behaviours we witness, enact, or tolerate, which mean nothing or seem innocuous to us, can have serious negative repercussions on others.

My parents taught us to be respectful of others. I vividly remember my father going out of his way to show me a stunning photograph on the cover of a magazine, an Inuit woman holding her baby close to her face, almost nose to nose. "Look at that mother's face and the love she has for her baby,

Kim. People are the same wherever they come from - a mother's love is universal." I idolized my father, and his words had an impact. Even today, when I hear about the atrocities in war-torn countries and see images of refugees, my mind goes to the mothers who love their children as much as I love mine.

People are the same. It was a long time before I understood that thinking people are the same should not be confused with saying one does not 'see' colour or the differences between us. Those differences can be celebrated and honoured.

But I found it difficult to reconcile Dad's message about what we have in common as human beings with the comments he made on another occasion when he expressed outrage on behalf of a friend whose daughter had married a Japanese man. "How could she do that?" he asked. I was aghast at his opinion. I pushed back. He would disown me, he responded, if I ever married outside my race.

Anyone who knew Dad, when they hear this story, state he would not have done that. But a war in which the Japanese were the enemy had impacted his worldview. A system that erased the truth of the Indigenous in our country educated him – and his children. Our society perpetuated the stereotype of 'drunk Indians'. We lived in a country where we thought racial problems existed only south of the border, in the United States. We were ignorant of what was behind our own government's Indian Act or the treatment of Black people and Asian people who lived within our borders. I was an adult before I learned Canada turned away a ship of Jews from its borders in 1939, condemning those on board to the fate of concentration camps.

And I'm sad to say, these racist attitudes are not reflective of just our past. Our present contains many who hold on to these beliefs, refusing to listen, learn, and evolve.

Martin Luther King Jr. dreamed of a time when people "will not be judged by the color of their skin, but by the content of their character."

I wish I could write that his dream has been realized. Perhaps by including this essay, I can encourage us to do better, to recognize racism, to see our differences and not feel threatened by them, and then to go a step further by accepting and even celebrating them. I encourage us to walk with our Indigenous people to learn the truth and to reconcile so we can move into a better future for all. Yes, Every Child Matters. Yes, Black Lives Matter. Until we achieve equality, no, we can't say all lives matter.

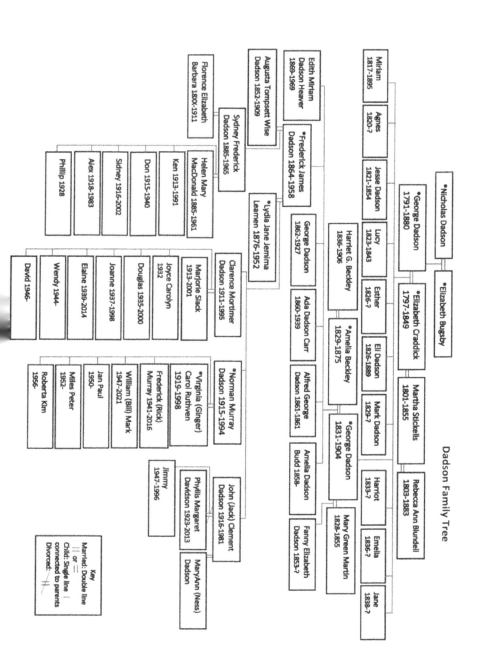

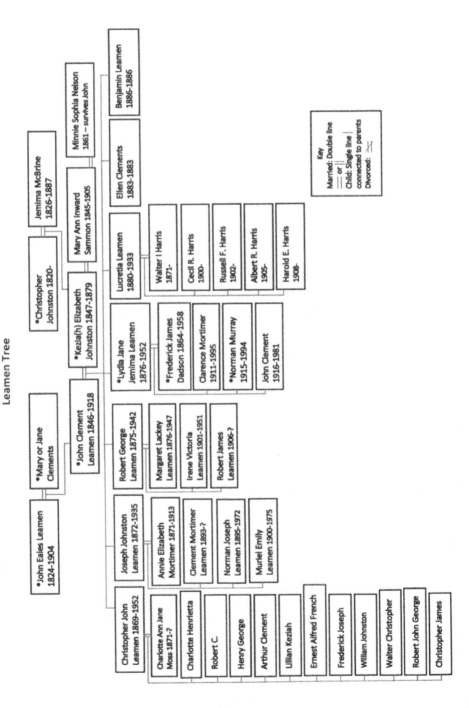

Leamen Tree

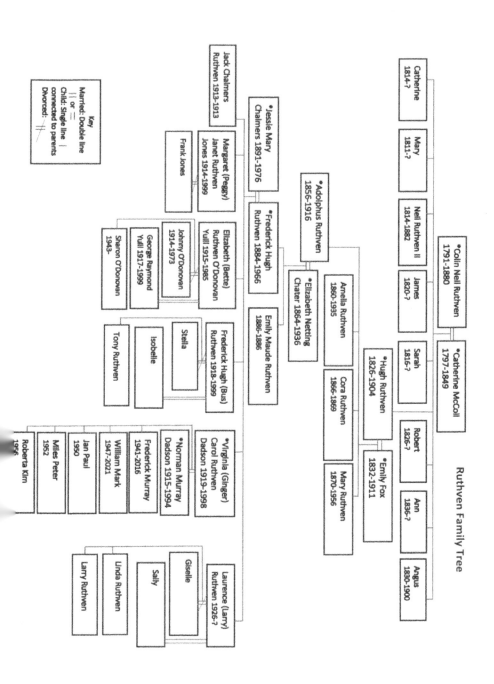

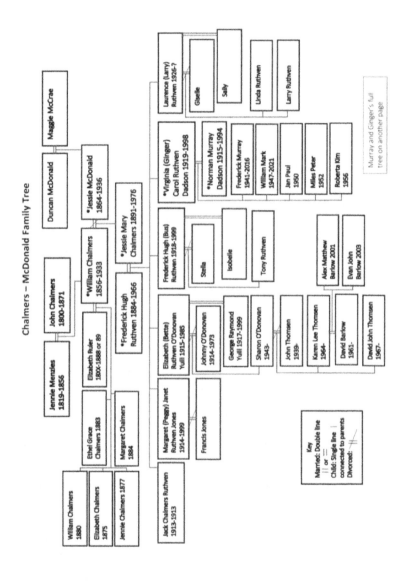

Chalmers – McDonald Family Tree

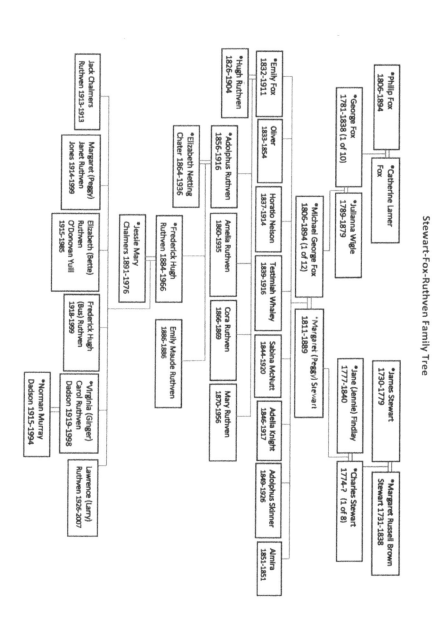

Stewart-Fox-Ruthven Family Tree

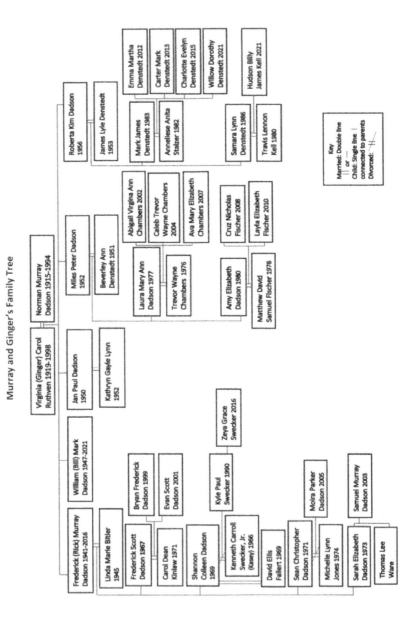

Murray and Ginger's Family Tree

Ginger's Restaurant

Pork Barbecue

Mom served this at the rehearsal dinner parties the nights before Jan and Miles were married. Mom and Dad hosted these events in their home, and they served this buffet style with pickles, coleslaw, and potato chips. Eat like a hamburger or you can serve it open-face style on a bun.

Ingredients

2 tbsp. butter	1 small onion, chopped
1 garlic, chopped	2 cups boiling water
2 tbsp. flour	1 tsp red pepper
2 tbsp. chili powder	1/8 teaspoon cayenne pepper
1 teaspoon mustard	1 teaspoon salt
1/4 cup Worcestershire sauce	1/4 cup vinegar
1 small bottle ketchup	3 1/2 to 4lbs loin pork, bone in

Directions

Melt butter with onion and garlic, add flour, then water. Add rest of seasoning, then meat. Cook slowly for two or more hours. Tear/shred meat from the bone and cook another hour or so. Red pepper and cayenne pepper are optional, depending on how hot you like it.

Curried Fruit

This is an excellent side dish to serve with ham or turkey. It's a nice make-ahead dish.

Ingredients

1/2 cup butter	3/4 cup brown sugar
4 teaspoon curry powder	1 large can of fruit salad
Jar of maraschino cherries	1 can pineapple chunks

Directions

Day before: Heat oven to 325 degrees. In an oven-proof casserole, melt butter and add sugar and curry. Drain and dry the canned fruit. (After using the colander to drain the fruit, Mom used to put this on a paper towel and sop as much juice off the fruit as possible.) Place and mix fruit in the casserole. Bake for one hour. Next day: reheat before serving.

Mince and Tatties

Mom never called this dish by this name - I believe we called it Hash or Hamburger Hash. It was a simple meal when hamburger was a budget meat to serve a family. It was also a very tasty "comfort" meal on cold nights.

Ingredients

1 pound hamburger	1 onion
Water	Salt and pepper to taste
Potatoes	

Directions

Heat the hamburger and onion in a large pot on the stove top. Once browned, add salt and pepper, and then add water, around 2 - 3 cups. If you prefer this a little thicker, bring it to boil and slowly add some mixed flour and water. Keep it simmering. Boil your potatoes in another pot and when ready, drain and mash them by hand, or whip them with a beater. Place a scoop of potatoes in the middle of the plate/bowl and with a spoon make a crater in the middle of them. Take a scoop of the hamburger and water and pour it into the crater and over the potatoes. Great served with ketchup and pickles. Add salt and pepper to taste.

Christmas Jell-O

This was always on the table at Christmas and Thanksgiving.

Ingredients

2 packages of grape Jell-O   Jar of pitted cherries

Directions

Make the Jell-O according to package directions. Pour into a mould. Slowly add the cherries distributing throughout the mould. Refrigerate. When set, carefully turn mould upside down onto the plate for serving.

Hard Sauce

This is very, very sweet but excellent when paired with tart-tasting mincemeat pie. Note: the measurements are approximate.

1-pound softened butter
Almond flavouring - about a teaspoon.
Enough icing sugar to mix with the butter, like an icing for cake, not overly soft.

When mixed, form into small logs, about 8 or so inches long, and two inches thick. Wrap in wax paper and freeze.

When ready to serve, remove and slice the logs into wafers, about 1/4 inch thick. Serve on warm mincemeat pie or tarts.

The Letters

Tues. Mar. 14 – 44

My Dear Ginger: –

I received your first letter to-day Hon and was I ever glad to hear from you. I know I should have written sooner, but all the time I was at Belleville I was expecting to get payed and have a forty-eight. I kept putting it off longer and longer, and when we finally got our clear and papers signed, I found out there was no pay coming and no time off. They had a pay day here to-day, but we are not officially on strength here, and so there will be no pay for us until the end of the month. When I do get payed, it will be a big one, because I am earning seventy-five cents a day flying pay now. I got a postcard in the mail to-night saying there is a parcel in the Express Office in Belleville waiting for me. You mentioned in your letter that you sent me a birthday parcel. Could that be it? I have no way of getting it. I tried the mail office to pick it up, but they only gave an excuse. I am taking night classes now, and besides, it costs fifty cents to ride to town. I guess the parcel will have to wait till the end of the month.

You called me down for not writing to you. You must remember that I have been dead broke, not even any smoking tobacco, and just sitting, waiting for these inefficient bastards to make up their feeble minds as to what they were going to do with us. I borrowed a dollar from a guy and now that's gone. I went to the post office three times a day at Belleville but didn't receive any mail.

March the seventh I spent just like the other days. In fact, I didn't know what day it was until it was time to turn in. I'm not complaining, Hon. Honest I'm not. I have just been bitched by the fickle finger of fate.

You say you were trying to get me on the phone. Well Hon all that barrack block is filled with "x" flight now. They are fellows who have finished their courses and are awaiting postings. None of that gang know me, and I was in a room upstairs at the opposite end of the building.

Right now, I feel like tearing this letter up Hon. I've reread it, and all it is is a list of complaints. I was really worried about you and Rick myself. You must remember this is about the fourth or fifth letter from me and to-day is the first I have heard from you. I am so glad to hear from you and yet I write a letter like this. I can't make it out.

I guess that parcel is from you, Hon. If it is, thanks a lot. I really don't need anything, though. We are well clothed and well fed. The only trouble is I am broke and will be until after my next forty-eight.

Don't take this letter to heart, Hon, and in your next letter, tell me again how much you love me. Try not to miss me so much, for we will not be seeing much of each other until this whole course is over. Have you got any coal left in the cellar. Don't forget you will have to pay for the next delivery. I will be able to send you some money at the end of the month. From there on things will be better. We start flying in a couple of weeks. All our flights will be bombing. We studied the bomb sight to-day, and are they ever intricate affairs. No wonder they cost so much. We will be doing half our flying at night and half by day. We drop all our bombs on targets in the lake. There is a block buster bomb on this station, and our instructor is going to show it to us some day. There was to be an Avro York come in here from Malton to-day, but it did not show up. It is a transport version of the Lancaster. I guess Bob Wingfield will be on it when it comes in. If he is, I hope I can get a ride.

I haven't been able to locate Harry Saville yet. I guess he must be on night duty. The planes are up night and day here. There is a continual roar. The other classes used to take up gunning in the air – like Larry; but we only shoot the machine gun on the ground and all our time in the air is spent on bombing. We will drop as many bombs on this course as a straight bomber.

I guess I will close now, Hon. I love you, you will never understand how much. I miss our little Rickey too. Keep your chin up Sweetheart, remember you'll have to be a mother and a father to him until I come home again. When you read this, please smile for me, and say to yourself "everything is all right, Murray is still crazy about me and thinks of us always."

I love you Sweetheart. I love you. I really do love you. Remember the night I first kissed you? Remember when I first spoke to you? Remember Long Branch Park on a warm summer evening? Remember how on such nights, I used to meet you, and take you home? Remember our first date, and the day I gave you your ring? Remember our wedding day and the following two weeks? I think of these often. I think of the time when Rickey was born, and you came home from the Hospital. I think of how you & Rickey sing songs together. I think of how beautiful you looked to me, when I kissed you good by the last time.

Don't ever write to me again and ask me whether I have forgotten you and Rick. I have so many fond memories and think so dam much of my family that it would be impossible to forget. Write again soon, Sweetheart.

Good night and kisses to you both. Murray

P.S. send some 4 stamps.

Sat. Mar. 15 – 44

My Darling: –

I have just now come away from our phone call Hon. It was great hearing you, and Ricky too. I could hear him more plainly than you Ging. As I was saying, we were twenty miles away from camp all day. We went down in a truck in the morning and came back about seven o'clock. We fired about five hundred bullets each from a four-gun turret. The four guns fire 80 rounds a second, so it only took five seconds of actual firing to get rid of them. Every fifth bullet was a tracer, and you could see them go through the target, hit the water, and skip away up in the air. The bullets cost ten cents each and when you press the firing button for one second, it costs eight dollars. Besides firing the guns, we set off some star signals, distress signals and the like. They were like huge skyrockets and burnt at about five hundred feet. The firecrackers were worth about twenty-five dollars. All in all, we spent about a thousand dollars' worth of ammunition in no time. No wonder they need to float another victory loan – eh? I guess by this time, Larry must have shot away a small fortune.

Since they cut out the air firing on this course, the classes have been getting a third 48. There has been no official word yet; but it seems likely we will get it.

I was at the show last night and saw that new picture called "Uninvited." It was a spooky picture about an old house in England. There is a good one on to-night with Orson Wells starring in it, but the exams start to-morrow. They get real good pictures here; some of them are hot off the press. I guess I make you mad – talking about going to the show, but I never go in Hon but what I don't wish you were with me.

I miss you Ging and love you always. The boys in our class often talk about their girls and wives. I was telling them to-day that before I was married, I thought I was madly in love with you; but it was nothing compared to the feeling I have now. The other married men agreed with me. (I guess you think I have gone nuts) But don't you feel different now, Hon? The longer I know you, the more I love you. That does not mean I wasn't in love with you before. Christ I'm getting in too deep here. I'll explain it when I get home; but I do love you Ging ever so much.

If this weather keeps up like this, I think we will have to move to California after the war – or maybe the West Indies. How would you like that, Hon? I am not fooling, I mean it. I'm not going to shiver my ass off all my life.

It's getting kind of late Hon. I want to have a shave and a wash and get into bed. There is no sleeping in in the morning here, and if you're tired the only thing to do is go to bed earlier. Ho-Hum- pardon me? I'm getting sleepy. I'll be seeing you, Hon. I love you and miss you. Take care of yourself and Rick and <u>don't work too hard.</u>

I love you
I love you
I love you
I love you
I love you
Murray

Thur. Mar. 16 – 44
Dear Ginger: –
I did not write last night Hon but phoned instead. It sure was nice to hear your voice. Your mail seems to be coming into me regularly now Sweetheart. Keep the good work up. The letter I got this morning was written on Tuesday night. You wrote that Jeremy sprained his ankles – how is he getting along? How is little Ricky doing these days. I miss him a lot Hon.

All the roads down here are covered with ice. It's one of those days.

Because of the weather all the planes are grounded. We spent all morning on the range. I was firing a rifle that was made at Small Arms and a John English machine gun. Do we ever eat up the ammunition with those machine guns. They fire twenty-five shots a second.

In the afternoon we had lectures on the bomb sight, and a class in aircraft recognition. Our aircraft rec. teacher is a sergeant W.D. There is a big dance going on in the drill hall now. It is just across the road from our hut. The hostesses are up from Belleville to do this big dance here. I wish you and I could go to it. I miss you Hon. I am writing this letter in the Airman's lounge. Have I told you about it yet? It is the size of one whole hut. There is a huge stone fireplace at one end. The furniture is really good. There are Chesterfields and Chesterfield chairs. All the lighting is from floor lamps like our big one. I am sitting next to the radio, writing this letter on some sort of a coffee table.

P.S. I love you Sweetheart. There is a fellow here who lives in New Toronto. I mentioned him to you before. His name is Joe Sutton. He is a nice-looking kid who used to work with Al Mckewan (sic) in the time office. He is going to drop in at the store and say hello to you. I am telling you this so you will know who he is. Don't worry, I'm not taking any chances. He's married and will have his wife with him. P.S. I love you.

How do you like working at the A&P? Don't do too much lugging around. You mentioned something about lugging things around in your last letter. How do they treat you over there? I guess you will be meeting people you know all day long. P.S. I love you.

Have you been up to see Mom and Pop lately. If you see them say hello from me. There is not much I could write them that would be of any interest. I know they like to see you and Rickey drop in on them.

I guess I will close now, Hon. I love you and you only. Good night Sweetheart. Kiss Ricky for me. I miss you both.

Loads of kisses & all my love
Murray

Thursday Mar. 23
My Dear Wife: –
Hello Sweetheart, how's about a kiss? What are you doing to-night?

See? I miss you. I received a letter from you to-day Hon, and boy was it ever welcome. What's the idea of working so hard? Take it easy over in that store. And another thing don't go tiring yourself out cleaning up the house just before I come home. Just leave it Hon, and I'll fix it up for you. I mean that now. There is a big dance on the station to-night. There will be three busloads of beautiful Belleville Hostesses, supplemented, of course, by our own W. D's. to entertain the boys. We spent half the afternoon to-day in gun turrets. They are rigged up in a building and are equipped with camera guns. We had to shoot at moving pictures of aeroplanes. I was thinking of Larry all the time I was in them. He certainly has to know his stuff, and be damn good, and I'm not kidding.

It won't be long Hon until I am home again for a short while. See I miss you. Where will we be going Tuesday night? We always have a good time with the Maceys and the Crosses. I wonder if the Park will be open on Tuesday night? We always seem to have a good time up there – don't we? You mentioned in your letter that I should drop in on the Dobbies. Does that mean you will be there? When I get in at the station, I will phone home and find out where you are. I hate bothering you like this Hon; but – do you still love me?

We have nearly finished our groundwork and will be ready to fly to-morrow. It will be a lot better when we have flying time to put in. Wasn't it a dull day to-day? The weather always (sic) reflects on me. When it is gloomy, so am I, and when it's bright it makes me feel good. Say Ging I could give you a blow-by-blow description of a love scene from where I am writing this letter. There is a young W.D. and an airman sitting on a chesterfield right next to me. I wish it were you and I. They are both very dark and small; so, I guess they must be French, but they are talking, speaking English. She keeps fussing with his hair and buggering about. I guess they must be in love – eh? They just got up and left. I guess they went to the dance. Bing Cosby has just come on the radio, and I love you.

Here comes Joey, the kid from New Toronto. He works over on the gun turrets where I spent the afternoon. He just borrowed my nail file, and I still love you.

There's nothing much to write about around here Hon, and I guess you are tired of reading "I love you". The lnk Spots are singing

"Stormy Weather", and I'm thinking of home. I don't know what I'll do when I go down to New Brunswick. I love my wife. I love our baby Ricky, and oh' how I miss them. The lounge is rather empty now. I guess most of the gang are up at the dance.

I guess, when the war is over and I come home again, we will get used to each other again and forget about these lonely nights. Or will we Hon? I love you more now than I ever have.

Did you make a mistake when you married me Hon? Are you sorry? I know I have left you with a lot of worry and responsibility and it bothers me. I will owe you so much by the time I get back, that it will take all my life to repay.

P.S. I love you Hon. How about a buck-tooth-kiss?

Later on, I'm going to polish my brass and have a shower; then lay on my bunk and think of you. I don't know a better way of spending an evening, since I can't come home to you. Do you realize you are impeding the war effort. The instructor has to wake me up and bring me back to Mountain View every once in a while. I'm always daydreaming, and you are always in my dreams.

This will be the last letter before my forty-eight. You will get it on Saturday. There will be no mail Sunday, and I will be home Monday.

Now don't go working yourself to a frazil around the house. Take it easy and be ready to go out and enjoy yourself. I'll fix things up for you when I get home.

I love you for many things, among them the many fond memories. I think of the silly little things we used to do together, and they seem so important to me now. I love you Hon. It's getting late so I guess I'll have to go. Good night, Dear. I'll be seeing you soon.

Yours always, Murray

P.S. I guess you think I'm nuts, but I do miss you Ging and never - never could I love anyone but you.

Mar. 31 - 44

My Dear Ginger.

I have just finished phoning home, and I was disappointed when you were not in. It is such a cold night Hon I was wondering if you had received your coal or not. I guess I will leave my phoning until (sic) from now on. It is only ten to eight. Sweetheart, will you hurry my watch along as fast as possible. I need it badly. Nink's watch is absolutely no good at all. There was no flying for our class to-day on account of the low clouds. We were going to do low level bombing from a thousand feet, but the clouds come down just before we took off. We were in the plane on the runway when the control tower signaled us to come back.

I sent five dollars in the last letter and there will be five in this one. I will send home fifteen out of this pay; let me know if you received it or not.

I haven't told you yet how much I miss you Dear. Well, I do very, very much, and I love you more than you will ever know. I went to an extra night class in Aldis Laup just a little while ago. If the weather gets any better, we will be flying night and day to catch up on the flying time. I have only been up three times but have put in more hours than I did all the while I was at the Toronto Flying Club.

You said you were not well, just as I was leaving last Wednesday night. I hope you are feeling o.k. now, Hon. I wish I was home to help you when you are feeling low like that. I do love you so much.

There will be exams coming up in a week or so, and I will have to study a bit. If I don't find time to write, I will phone you instead. Gosh, I wish you were home when I phoned a while ago. I wanted to hear your voice. I feel down in the dumps to-day. I guess the weather has something to do with it, too. But the weather will surely break soon; and then everything will seem brighter. I really have so much to be thankful for, I shouldn't be feeling blue.

I will sign off now Hon and go back to my bunk to get a little study done. Don't forget the watch Hon. Send it in a large enough box so that it doesn't get lost in the mail.

Goodnight, Dear. I'll be seeing you again soon – I hope.

Yours always, Murray

P.S. Give Rick a big hug and kiss for me and oodles of love and kisses to you. I love you, I love you, I love you.

Sun. 23/4/44

My Darling Ginger: –

Remember me? I'm the guy who pops in and pops out again every once in a while. We didn't get into camp until four thirty this morning. The train had a "hot box" and stopped every little once in a while. There was lots of room however, and the coaches were first class, and we were able to sleep most of the time. Denny and I ate the sandwiches about ten thirty this morning. I was up low-level bombing by eight thirty. I missed breakfast to get to briefing in time, so we ate the lunch when we came down. I won't get payed until Friday Hon, but I will send some money as soon as I get it.

The exams started to-day. They are all oral exams, but I haven't been called in yet. One of these days I am going to forget to get off the train myself. What do you think! Last night I left my pipe on the train. I am in the lounge now; Hon. Jack Benny has just finished. This is Dennis Day's last program. He is going into the Navy.

I wonder if Larry is home yet. Don't forget to tell him to write me; and let me know all about his aircraft and crew. How was Rick when he woke up this morning? I suppose he was a hand full to-day, seeing as how it is raining out and he had to stay indoors. Denny wanted to know how you and Rick were. He is worrying about his low bombing scores and told me not to mention them to you. He says he's cheesed off this damn bombing chore.

I haven't told you yet, Hon, but I love you. Every time I come back from a forty-eight, I go around in a daze. Even when I close my eyes, I see you. It's just Ginger – Ginger – Ginger. It takes a couple of days before I can get back in the groove.

When we were up this morning, we dropped out bombs early and went for a side up through the clouds. We met a Harvard and chased it around for a while. I only have three or four more trips to make before I am finished.

I will close now, Hon. Don't work too hard at your new job. Remember that I still love you and always will. So long for now, Sweetheart. I'll write again to-morrow night. I love you and miss you.

Good-night Darling

Murray

Tue. 25/4/44

Hi Hon.

How are you to-night? I received a letter from you to-day, and by the way, how come you thought I was mad when I left the last time? I phoned last night, and you were at the show, and I wasn't the least bit disappointed. This is the truth Hon, I was glad to know that you were out to the show enjoying yourself. By the way – I love you, Ging.

There was an "Air-cobra" over here yesterday. He was stunting all over the place. He was a test pilot and has a brother on the station. The control tower personnel wanted to report him for diving down on the runways, but he had no numbers on and was a U.S. craft. Bill used to use a lot of them at Niagara. Do you remember him telling us about them?

Has Larry come home yet? Don't forget to get him to write me. To-morrow we go down to the Y.M.C.A and have dingy drill in the swimming pool. That ought to be a lot of fun.

Denny and I are talking all the while about what we are going to do on our 48's at the coast. We intend to rent a boat. He is quite a sailor at heart and enjoys swimming and boating.

There is still a strong chance, Hon, that I will not finish this course. My Aldis is improving, but it is far from up to the standard they want it to be. I don't know whether I would be C.T.'d all together or sent on to some other course in air crew. Since I have come to this station, my attitude has changed, and I don't seem to worry about passing or not. Don't you worry about it Hon, I just wanted to let you know how things are.

It is getting late Dear, so I will sign off. Good-night Ginger.

I love you – that is one thing I will never slacken up in – my love for you and Rick.

Good nite Darling
Murray.

Tue. 18/4/44

My Darling: –

This is my first letter in three days, and I am ashamed of myself; but as an excuse, I must say I have been kept busy. We were flying last night, and the night before, and in between there have been classes, and the exams are right upon us. I am in the classroom now. It is now ten a.m., and I have just got out of bed. The class is starting now Hon, so I will sign off for an hour or so.

Hello Hon. I am on my lunch hour. I have been down to the P.O.

There was no letter to-day; but I received one from you yesterday. You mentioned the fact that you might stop work. I hope you do Hon. If I get through this course o.k, I will be able to send you more money. If I don't, I will be set back to an a so if you will wait for a few weeks and then we will know. I love you.

Hasn't the weather been good these last two days? It makes me think back to the time we had together on such bright days. Our 48 is in the bag, Hon; so, I will be seeing you Thursday night.

We had a contest on last night with our bombing. There was a bad wind given to us by the met. officer, and all our scores were bad. Mine were not so bad; but not good enough to win. We all put in ten cents and the best score took the pot.

We have been studying bombs lately. We have to do practical work with them and set them up for the aircraft. There are classes this afternoon and flying again to-nite.

I have not got much time now, Hon. I'll sign off now and mail this letter.

I love you and miss you. You are forever in my thoughts. Give Ricky a hug and kiss for me and tell him his Daddy will be home soon.

I love you
Murray

Mon. 24/4/44
My Darling: –
I am writing this letter on my bunk, so if the words seem jumbled and jivey, please excuse same. I had four exams to-day Hon, and to-morrow I will get a few more off my chest. I have just come from the barber shop and after I write this letter, I am going to have a wash and get into bed. I am wondering how you made out at Campbell's to-day? Hasn't it been a bitch of day – rain, rain, rain.

I was talking to Harry Saville to-day. He was the orderly officer, and I met him in the mess hall. I think he has just returned from leave. I just borrowed some change; so, I think I will phone you. It is now a quarter to nine. You ought to be home.

This will only be a short note, Hon. Everything is o.k. here, except that I miss you so much.

I want to tell you how much I miss you and how much I care, but the words just don't seem to come. Don't forget to let me know about Larry as soon as you can and send the pictures when you get them, and I will send them back.

I love you
I miss you
Murray

Aug. 2 1944
Darling Ginger: –
Hello Hon – how be you? I'm sorry about not writing last night, but we were supposed to fly, and then at the last minute it was washed out. We have been slated to fly five times this week and each time it has been washed out. Our last trip was July 19th.

I received your letter to-day in which you were asking me about getting some time off. I'll have to find out what they think of it here first. So, wait until you hear from me. I'll have to talk with Flt/Lt Duffy to-morrow.

After supper tonight a bunch of us went down swimming. We bummed a ride on a sailing sloop too. It was lots of fun.

You did want to know when this course finished. It is September the 22nd. That is a Friday, and I will be home on Saturday September the 23rd.

I can't seem to write to-night Hon. It's so damned hot here, I'm soaked through. I hope you're not working in this heat. Take care of yourself, sweetheart. Remember, I still love you and miss you more than ever.

So long for now, Hon
Love Murray

Friday Aug. 4 1944
My Dear Wife: –
Do you realize that the moon rises to-night at fourteen minutes after midnight G.M.T.

Pardon me, I'm just "gearing" up for to-night's flip. We have to have all that dope in our logs when we go flying.

I was talking to F/L Duffy today. He told me I wouldn't be able to get any time off. So, I guess those six weeks are out of the question,

Hon. I received a letter from you to-day, and the pictures you took up at Mom's. Haven't Pete and Marge got fat lately?

Say Hon! It's nine o'clock now, and briefing is in half an hour. I'll have to go over to the barracks and get my parachute harness and maps. I'll write some more when I come down. So long for now, Sweetheart. I love you.

Hallo again Hon. Here I am in the classroom. It is just past ten o'clock a.m. We had quite a trip last night. Jack Heaton was first navigator, and I was second nav. Our first timing point was Charlottetown P.E.I. and from there we went southeast to a position in the Bay of Fundy. From the Bay of Fundy, we came almost due north to the base. We took off at half-past eleven and set course over Newcastle at a quarter to midnight. There have been so many forest fires lately that it made it hard to use the ground. However, once we were out over the water, the air became clearer, and with a big moon directly in front of us, map reading became easier.

As I said before, I was second nav. and all I had to do was pinpoint myself every ten minutes or so and take sextant shots of the moon and stars.

It was a grand trip up until we started on our last leg. Over the Bay there was fog covering nearly everything and when the fog cleared out, as we got farther inland, the smoke from the forest fires took its place. We flew on one course for nearly an hour without seeing a light or the ground. Heaton must have been hot last night; because on our E.T.A we were only a mile away from Newcastle.

Some of the pilots, we learned on landing, had turned back earlier because of the poor visibility. Well, so much for the navigation Sweetheart.

How are you this morning? We are taking up compass swings now; but we have taken them so many times that I figure I know all about it now. Big-headed, eh.

I'll sign off now, Sweetheart. We have to go over for a period of dots and dashes now.

I love you. I love you. I love you.

So long for now, Hon.

Your Murray

Roberta Kim

Thursday Aug. 10 1944
  Darling Ginger: –
  Hello Hon, how be you? I received two letters from you to-day, and were they good to get. We had our flip last night, and it wasn't until daylight before we went to bed. We were to fly this afternoon; but when we got up, we were told to put on old clothes and get ready to fight a bush fire. So, the whole class has been hard at it all afternoon. The fire was caused by practice bombs on the Logieville target. The target is in the middle of a cedar swamp, and the fire was burning mostly underground. You know how the two fall down in a swamp and the earth is covered with dead wood, p??k and moss.
  The reason for putting it out was to stop it spreading into the thick bush. It had broken through in a few places the day before. The only thing we could do was to put out any small fires that sprung up in the bush. We had to carry big haversacks, strapped on our backs. The haversacks are waterproof and have a hosepipe and a pump attached to the bottom. You carry the sack on your back and hold the pump in your hands. Do you follow me? Do you love me? I love you. Oh! So much.
  Well to get back to the fire. The CO and our own two officers came with us. The C.O. is one grand fellow. He didn't take the water bag off his back all day, and it is heavy, holding three pails of water. I was all in after two or three trips, and I handed my bag over to one of the relief fellows. We had a gasoline engine pump and over a mile of hose line. The fire will not be out until it rains, and rains down hard.
  I am glad to hear that you and Rickey have had a day out at the Port. Henry and Helen are the best of friends, and I just know you must have had an enjoyable time. I suppose Betty is all over her appendix operation.
  Ginger about me getting 6 weeks off after I finish the course here. I understand that, but F/Lt Duffy told me it couldn't be done. You must remember that even if I did get a wing here, I wouldn't be a full-fledged navigator. There is still about nine more months of training before I could go on ops. He told me I would be still under training for months after I graduate here.
  Well Sweetheart it's nearly eleven o'clock, and I'm dead tired. To-day I did the first day's work since I left Campbells Soup, and I am

tired.

I love you, miss you, and want you with every breath I take. I'll be seeing you to-morrow night.

Love Murray

P.S. Tell Rick the 3 of us will have "pupper" on the train someday.

Sunday Aug. 13 1944

Darling Ginger: –

It is early Sunday afternoon. I just got up in time to get my dinner. I am going down to the river for a swim in a little while, so I'll post this letter in town. We have to fly tonight on an astro trip, and I am first navigator. It is another long trip down to the border, and on one of the digs I have to navigate by Radio.

We write our first final exam next Wednesday. It is on photography, and ought to be easy. After this week, I'll have to start studying. I love you, Hon.

Say Ginger one thing I wanted to ask you. Who made those socks that were in the bundle I got? Are they the ones that Miss Galloway made for me?

I am pleased to learn that you had a Port. Is Bette Dobbie all over her operation now? How did Rickey behave on the beach? Did he go in the water? Are you still working, and if so, who is looking after Rickey? You haven't mentioned much about Bus and Larry lately. Where are they, and how are they doing?

It has been terribly hot lately, and I have been worrying about you working in this heat. Do take care of yourself, Ging. I wish you would give it up. This will only be a short note. I don't feel much like writing now; but I promise you a good letter later on. Give Rickey a big hug and kiss for me. I love you both and miss you terribly. I'll be home in a month's time.

So long for now

Murray

P.S. I love you.

References

1. *Adams, John Coldwell, Confederation Voices: Seven Canadian Poets*
2. *Beaton, Joyce, I Be Two in 'Tember, 2005*
3. *Beaton-Bihari, Joyce, The Dadsons of Cranbrook and Canada, 2014*
4. *Beaton, Joyce, Finding Father's Family, 2000*
5. *Beers & Co., J.H., Commemorative Biographical Record of the County of Essex, 1905.*
6. *Bliss, Carman: https://citas.in/autores/bliss-carman/*
7. *Burch, Mrs. Mary J., "A Family Record," Windsor, Ontario, 1880, pages 79 to 85, posted by James Shearer to Ancestry*
8. *Canada, Arriving Passenger Lists, 1865-1935*
9. *Canadian Immigration, https://www.british-immigrants-in-montreal.com/ canadian-immigration-early-1900s.html*
10. *Christian, Ellen, Confessions of an Overworked Mom, The Legend of the Bayberry Candle and History https://confessionsofanover-worked Mom.com/ the-legend-of-the-bayberry-candle/*
11. *Cranbrook and District Local History Society, Cranbrook, A Wealden Town*
12. *Digital History, Torches of Freedom Campaign, https://biblio.uottawa.ca/omeka2/jmccutcheon/exhibits/show/america n-women-in-tobacco-adve/torches-of-freedom-campaign*
13. *Family Search.org*
14. *Freeman, Ruth and Klaus, Patricia, Journal of Family History, 1984.*
15. *Friedman, Ann, Book Review on The Social Sex: A History of Female Friendship" by Marilyn Yalom and Theresa Donovan Brown, New York Times. New York Times: https://www.nytimes.com/2015/ 09/20/books/review/the-social-sex-a-history-of-female-friendship.html*
16. *Gray, Charlotte, The Massey Murder A Maid, Her Master and the Trial that Shocked a Country.*
17. *Grodzinski, John R., Vronsky, Peter, McIntosh, Andrew, Fenian Raids, The Canadian Encyclopedia, https://www.thecanadian encyclopedia.ca/en/article/fenian-raids, 2021*
18. *Gjenvick-Gjonvik Archives website. https://www.gjenvick.com/OceanTravel/Brochures/AllanLine-1908-SecondCabinAccommodations.html*
19. *Harville Hendrix PH.D., Getting the love you want*
20. *Hong, A.G., Indoor Bowling, https://www.thecanadianencyclopedia. ca/en/article/indoor-bowling, 2013.*

21. *Irish quotes: https://www.highonsms.com/51148/quotes/irish-quotes-and-proverbs/wings-love-molt-feather*

22. *Kent and Sussex Courier, 1904*

23. *Klein, Christopher, An Irish-American Army Invaded Canada in 1866. Here's What Happened, Time.com, March 2019*

24. *National Archives - https://www.nationalarchives.gov.uk/currency-converter/#currency-result*

25. *Norway Heritage, SS Corsican, Allan Line www.norway heritage .com*

26. *Queen Mary II: https://www.seat61.com/queen-mary-2transatlantic. htm*

27. *Norway Heritage Hands Across the Sea: http://www.norwayheritage.com/p_shiplist.asp?co=allan*

28. *Oxford Dictionary https://www.oxfordlearnersdictionaries.com/ definition/english/iconoclast*

29. *Poetry Foundation, My Last Duchess by Robert Browning, https://www.poetry foundation.org/poems/43768/my-last-duchess*

30. *Ramsay, Edward: https://quotefancy.com/quote/1774455/Edward-Ramsay-May-the-hinges-of-friendship-never-rust-nor-the-wings-of-love-lose-a- feather*

31. *Scotia Bank Family History Centre*

32. *Swider, B., Harari, D., Breidenthal, A.P., Bujold Steed, L. Perfectionism according to research, Harvard Business Review https://hbr.org/2018/12/the-pros-and-cons-of-perfectionism-according-to-research*

33. *The Wiffenpoofs, https://en.wikipedia.org/wiki/The_Whiffenpoofs; https://www.whiffenpoofs.com*

34. *Thomas, Dylan, Do not go gentle into that good night, https://en.wikipedia.org/wiki/Do_not_go_gentle_into_that_good_night*

35. *Writers and Company, Eleanor Wachtel, Interview with Ian McEwan. October 20, 2022.*

36. *Wright, Giles R., Afro-Americans in New Jersey, A Short History, retrieved April 2021: https://nj.gov/state/historical/ assets/pdf/ topical/afro-americans-in-nj-short-history.pdf*

Roberta Kim

Made in the USA
Las Vegas, NV
07 May 2023

71729105R00168